Legacy of Wisdom

Legacy of Wisdom

GREAT THINKERS AND JOURNALISM

John C. Merrill

Iowa State University Press / Ames

John C. Merrill is professor emeritus of journalism
at the University of Missouri—Columbia.

♾ Printed on acid-free paper in the United States of America

First edition, 1994

Library of Congress Cataloging-in-Publication Data

Merrill, John Calhoun

Legacy of wisdom : great thinkers and journalism / John C. Merrill.—1st ed.

p. cm.

ISBN 0-8138-2041-3

1. Journalistic ethics. 2. Journalism—Philosophy. 3. Philosophers—Biography. 4. Philosophy. I. Title.

PN4756.M385 1994

174′.9097—dc20 94-14357

THIS BOOK IS LOVINGLY DEDICATED TO MY GRANDCHILDREN:

Erin

Brett

Susanna

Jack

Dorothy

Leah

&

Haley

CONTENTS

PROFILES

PROLOGUE

The great thinkers profiled briefly on the following pages have ideas that are especially valuable to today's journalists. They offer journalism and those who will practice it, or who do practice it, a great legacy of wisdom. Most attention in this book is given to the ethical ideas of these thinkers, not because these writers did not deal with other philosophical and practical matters of interest to the journalist, but because an ethical or moral foundation is direly needed in today's journalism.

From out of the intellectual mists of antiquity come the voices of provocative thinkers, their words—if listened to—capable of instilling in journalists a host of foundational concepts valuable to their thought and work. Such thinkers as Lao-tzu, Confucius, Plato, and Aristotle, although casting their broad nets far beyond journalism's special interests, manage to provide useful concepts for the practicing journalist or the wisdom-seeking student. And more recently, the journalist can contemplate the ideas of Machiavelli, Kierkegaard, Milton, Montaigne, Mill, Kant, and Schopenhauer. Then, perhaps speaking more directly and specifically to journalists today, are voices such as those of Karl Marx, Dietrich Bonhoeffer, Marshall McLuhan, Eric Hoffer, Ayn Rand, Barbara Tuchman, and Sissela Bok.

The journalist would do well to pause and listen to these voices. Whether getting ready to practice journalism or practicing it now, the journalist is fortunate to have available this legacy of wisdom easily adaptable to the pluralistic orientations existing in journalism. What is most important to the eclectic reader is the possibility that even from "ideological enemies" he or she can glean useful and stimulating concepts that can be integrated into a growing personal philosophy.

This wisdom-imbued legacy contains a wide variety of philosophic stances. The mild collectivists, the democratic socialists, the communitarians (who might be drawn to such figures as Plato, Rousseau, Marx, or Rawls) will find support in these profiles; the basically traditional, mixed-ideology, or dialectical conservatives will find comfort in the ideas of Confucius, Aristotle, and Voltaire; and another group of readers—the social engineers of various hues—can get some intellectual nourishment from most of these thinkers (except perhaps from the individualists and existentialists such as Rand and Kierkegaard).

Some of these thinkers might be considered more collectivist (for example, Plato) than individualist (Aristotle); more pessimistic (Schopenhauer) than optimistic (McLuhan); more liberal (Rawls) than conservative (Hoffer); more socially oriented (Hutchins) than personally oriented (Rand); more legalistic (Kant) than relativistic (Hume); more existentialist (Beauvoir) than rationalist (Locke); more pragmatically oriented (Machiavelli) than ethically oriented (Bonhoeffer); more mystical and non–language-oriented (Lao-tzu) than linguistically realistic (Korzybski); and more altruistic and consequence-driven (Mill) than "duty-driven" (Kant).

Obviously the above representation of specific thinkers and their philosophical inclinations is simplistic; each of the people in this volume is infinitely more complex than such labels can indicate. But these thinkers represent basic concepts that are appropriate for serious consideration by anyone interested in the practice of modern journalism. Basic defining labels, however unsatisfactory they may be in getting at the essence of a person, are somewhat useful—if not essential—in dealing with the complex world of philosophical, social, religious, and cultural concepts and the people who espouse or embrace them.

Some readers will consider this book somewhat gender-biased (only a few women are included) and slanted toward a Western and white ethnocentrism (most of the thinkers are European men). But to date, the people who have most influenced

American thinking, especially in epistemology, political philosophy, and ethics (the areas of most concern to journalists), have mostly been men of the Euro-American world. It is out of the thought of Western Civilization that American journalism has sprung. Perhaps if such a book as this is published 50 years from now, the situation will have changed, and significantly more races and world regions will be represented and more women will have had important lessons to share with the journalistic community.

This small book is meant to provide teachers, students, and journalists with introductions to some of the world's most stimulating and significant minds. These thinkers will be presented chronologically, beginning with the ancient Chinese and Greek sages. Naturally, many other people could have been included here, but a selection had to be made, and in this selection the reader will have a significant sample of the great thinkers of the world, from Confucius and Socrates to John Rawls and Iris Murdoch at the end of the 20th century.

The focus in these profiles is on ideas—mainly related to ethics—that are adaptable and significant to journalists and journalism/communications students. So taking this into consideration, along with the brevity of each sketch, it is inevitable that these profiles will have gaps in them. I make no apology for providing the reader with only a brief glimpse of these complex thinkers in hopes that he or she will be encouraged to seek a further acquaintance with some them.

The reader should understand that this book is in many ways a primer—and one, by the way, that is not dressed in the usual academic or scholarly garb—intended to be useful primarily to the novitiate's entry into the world of the great thinkers. The profiles are intentionally short; they are written so there is no need for footnotes, as biographical data and ideas are trimmed to their basics; they are written in a serious, but not heavy, scholarly form designed to invite further investigation by including for the reader the most significant books by each of the thinkers.

I hope that these profiles will offer valuable guidance and inspiration to journalists and journalism students seeking motivation in their professional lives. Although I am indulging in considerable interpretation, I hope that I am not going too far afield and that the projections of basic ideas to journalism are reasonable and that the inferences and conclusions will serve as catalysts to continued study. It is possible, perhaps probable, that some ideas presented in each profile have been imprecisely or erroneously interpreted and applied to the practice of journalism. If the reader feels uncomfortable with some of these ideational adaptations, he or she should feel free to make others more suitable to personal interpretation. At the very least, I feel that the fascinating and complex personalities introduced on the following pages will provide an intellectual springboard from which the serious reader can dive into much deeper and invigorating waters.

Acknowledgments

My wife, Dorothy, deserves special thanks for her help in critically reading, and initially editing, the manuscript of this book. I should also like to thank Jessie Dolch for her excellent copyediting. Also especially helpful in the development of the book were the following graduate students of mine at the University of Missouri: Terri Catlett, Anelia Dimitrova, Nileeni Meegama, and Fred Blevens.

Other journalism graduate students who, in their classes, contributed various insights to the profiles were Jesse Sam, Wendy Bell, Sau Chan, James Kropp, Jeff Reisner, Lane Barnholtz, Alison Boggs, Chris Allen, and Jennifer Davies.

I wish to thank also Professors Herb Strentz (Drake), Lou Hodges (Washington and Lee), Don Brenner (Missouri), Ralph Lowenstein (Florida), Jay Black (South Florida), Ralph Barney (Brigham Young), Dave Gordon (Emerson), and Howard Ziff (Massachusetts) for their encouragement and ethical insights shared with me over the years.

Legacy of Wisdom

[1]

CONFUCIUS

The great Chinese sage K'ung-Fu-tzu, or as we call him, Confucius, provides valuable guidance for one kind of journalism. Although, of course, Confucius (551–479 B.C.) did not deal with journalism per se, his overall philosophy and value system can easily be adapted to modern journalism. It can provide one perspective from which a journalist can develop an overall philosophy for his or her activities, especially for the person who is inclined toward a cooperative, adaptive, and socially involved kind of journalism. What is often called today "communitarian" journalism actually got its early impetus from Confucius.

Here was a foundational mentor who, in many ways, was similar in his ethical outlook (see his *Analects,* many editions) to two stalwarts of Western philosophy, Plato and Aristotle. In fact, he anticipated them and synthesized their respective emphases on collective loyalty and personal self-enhancement. Confucius, like Plato, was interested in harmonious personal adaptation to the group, and like Aristotle, he wanted to see a person develop intellectually and morally and to come to a high level of self-appreciation and self-realization.

For Confucius, like Aristotle, daily habitual activities in conformity with social customs—tempered with reason—formed the basis of morality and led to personal happiness and self-enhancement. But Confucius was more like Plato in that he would have journalists, for example, recognize that they are members of a group—a particular journalistic "family" or even a profession—and that each reaches moral maturity within that group.

The Confucian journalist would be loyal to that group—

that television station or newspaper. A spirit of cooperation and cohesion within the group is a basic Confucian precept. By and large, the ethics of the "society" (medium, group) become the ethics of the media functionary because a fundamental tenet of Confucianism is group loyalty and cooperation. This is illustrated when Confucius says that every person should be filial to parents and loyal to masters. In this respect, it could be said that Confucianist group loyalty and knowing one's place within the group is more akin to the ideas of Plato than to those of Aristotle.

At any rate, the Confucian journalist would be a cooperative and loyal member of the media organization, with ethical standards designed and determined largely by the social group and not individually. Tradition and past experiences of the organization (social group) would by and large determine the ethical perspective that the journalist would accept and follow.

As with modern communitarians, the weight of value is on the side of society (the social unit, the medium, or the profession). The journalist's work, for example, has meaning so far as it fulfills the role that it has been assigned within the social unit or profession. Therefore, the reporter is virtuous to the extent that he or she performs the duties of a reporter as determined by the medium or profession. The emphasis in Confucianism is on individual adaptation to the group, the community, and the society.

Social order was very important to Confucius, and order is preserved by customs and manners (*li*), which are imperatives of conduct. A person must adapt to the virtues (customs) of a society in order to become a true individual. The person must overcome self, said Confucius, and conform to the restrictions of *li*. When this happens, the person is moral and just. In all this, of course, learning is very important. Confucius believed that without learning, all virtues become vague and begin to dissolve; for example, without learning, bravery becomes foolhardiness or disobedience, frankness becomes rudeness or vulgarity, and firmness becomes obstinance or eccentricity.

History—especially those parts of history that evidence the nobility, creativity, and courage of certain human beings—was for Confucius a vital field of study. He called himself a traditionalist, one who was a faithful lover of the old. But as he examined the past, Confucius separated the good from the bad and selected facts that were worth remembering as models for human activity. It is safe to speculate that he would advise today's journalists to select for emphasis those stories that would reveal the nobility of the human being. A conservative demeanor? Perhaps, but Confucius sees such a conservative style of life always nourished and made dynamic by a liberalizing open-mindedness.

To be human is to communicate, and forthrightness and integrity in communication are essential. This was part of Confucius' basic wisdom. He also stressed as part of this wisdom that concern for others (*jen*) is not just a virtue but the core of all virtues. Confucius taught that a person should not be biased and that dogmatism is destructive of character. He saw the superior person as not being narrowly partisan but willing to look carefully at all sides, therefore preserving openness; such a person is firm in character, but not obstinate.

Confucius had a great respect for words but saw language as often misused. If words are not used correctly and with precision, judgments are unclear, and thinking goes awry. And what is more, this careless word-precipitated thinking will lead to wrong actions. He saw this as a basic stumbling block to good interpersonal relations. In this he anticipated the general semanticists of the 20th century and their leader, Alfred Korzybski. For Confucius, the superior person chooses words carefully and uses them with precision to bring about the kind of action desired. Imprecision in language usage was off limits for Confucius' superior person. He undoubtedly would say the same for today's journalist.

Confucius was no ascetic like his contemporary, Gautama the Buddha, but was a man of the world, involved in it, mixing thoroughly with others. In this he was quite different from both the Buddhists and Taoists (followers of Lao-tzu), who generally were believers of non-action and non-involvement. Lao-tzu taught that the *Tao* (the Way) could be revealed only by non-action, solitary meditations, and mystical experiences and that morality was grounded in this mystical *Tao*. Confucius, on the other hand, taught that social intercourse was necessary to a meaningful morality. It is hard to visualize Lao-tzu functioning in modern journalism, but Confucius—while scorning much of the substance of such journalism—could find a useful niche in it.

As to press freedom, Confucius would see its considerable limitations as a good thing. Realistic freedom must, for Confucius, have some moral grounding. A journalist should choose good, not evil; and if evil would prevail, then freedom would disappear. In the Confucian view freedom to choose is only freedom to choose good—not evil. For the modern journalistic context, freedom is freedom to be responsible, not irresponsible.

Hard work is another important foundation stone in Confucianism. The lazy journalist—the one who does not pull his or her weight, the one who procrastinates or shifts work to others—this journalist is exhibiting a fatal moral flaw. Work hard, be loyal, be cooperative, and have pride in the social unit: these are basic Confucian teachings.

Confucianism for the journalist would be an alternative to Western, especially Protestant, values of rugged individualism, sacrifice, and self-promotion. One can look at Japanese journalism, for example, to see that where Confucianism and Shintoism hold sway, the emphasis is not on individualistic values but rather on social conformity and group cooperation. So we can say that Confucian journalism has little affinity with Western liberal or individualistic journalism but in its basic outlook would be more akin to communitarianism, socialism, or a mild form of "soft authoritarianism."

Many Western journalists, steeped in the ideas of personal autonomy and libertarianism, will see great dangers in Confucian journalism. But it is simply a different way of looking at society and social institutions; in short, Confucian journalism emphasizes the unit or group, whereas modern Western liberal journalism enthrones the individual. Confucius saw the stability, dignity, and value of the social unit as taking precedence over the individual, and he saw the individual as taking personal worthiness from the group traditions and norms, rather than the other way around.

For the Confucian journalist, the "I" (so important to the American journalist) is sublimated to the "we"—the essential difference being the relative stress given to communitarian as opposed to individualistic values. Manners (*li*) are important; in fact, they play a key role in the daily ethical behavior of a person. Manners are socially concerned activities that show a concern for others and a certain respect for self as a part of society. Without manners, believed Confucius, life would be graceless and brutish. Ceremonial activities and predictable actions are a sign of respect for others and a key to moral living. Such everyday manners, according to Confucius, check undisciplined and ad hoc, often anti-social, behavior.

The Confucian journalist would act habitually, out of a sense of respect for others and a desire to stabilize the social situation. Virtues, for the Confucian journalist, can be learned and developed, becoming part of the person, and come into play naturally when needed to keep the person on the moral path: These things we do at our newspapers; these things we do not do. Action becomes almost automatic; there are no surprises for anyone.

Especially important in Confucian ethics are the virtues of work, courtesy, empathy, and consideration. There is this unwritten order of priorities for the Confucian journalist: respecting your elders and superiors, building up rather than tearing down, being positive rather than negative, always thinking of others and their problems, and being respectful—men to women, the able-bodied to the ill or crippled, the host to the guest.

Confucius provided a picture of what he considered the

"superior man," one who has a gentleman's manners and a sage's wisdom. Such a person (read: journalist) searches for the truth, investigates, asks critical questions, and seeks answers. The superior journalist, as opposed to the inferior one, is concerned with justice, not personal advancement and profit; is serene, not filled with anxiety; is congenial, never vulgar; dignified, not arrogant; steadfast, not flighty. The superior journalist tends to his or her own business, not the business of others; is slow in words and quick in action; and is concerned with the "here and now," the real worldly situation.

The Confucian journalist would think of others connected with a story. There would be no invasion of privacy, nothing that would bring shame or grief, no use of people as means to an end, no desire to "scoop" with superficial and hasty stories, no desire to make stories trivial, negative, or sensational in order to play to prurient interests of the audience. The Confucian journalist would want to expand the realm of rationality and civility, not the realm of titillation and bias. He or she also would want to maximize social harmony, not social friction; group cohesion, not group dissolution.

The Confucian journalist would accentuate the positive and de-emphasize the negative. Confucius would advise the journalist to recognize that human sympathy is more important than public disclosure, that humanistic considerations should take precedence over professional ones, that first of all the journalist is a person and secondarily a journalist. Confucius, some four centuries before Christ, proposed a kind of negative Golden Rule: you should not do unto others what you would not have others do unto you. This, like the Christian Golden Rule itself, would probably revolutionize journalism if it were practiced.

Confucius saw the entire social order structured and preserved by *li*—imperatives of conduct or manners that become customs. He drew no real distinction between custom and morality, between morality and justice. Custom, for him, embraced most activities of a person: his or her way of talking, of walking, of greeting others, of carrying on a conversation, and of behaving in company. And custom was directly connected to ethics. The customary way of acting was, for him, the ethical way of acting, and this carried over into the way work was governed. So the journalist would, qua journalist, follow the customs of his or her workplace, of the social norms governing those activities. When the journalist departed from these customary ways and struck out on an individual path, the social shell with its expectations would be broken, and the journalist would be acting unethically.

This is a much-abbreviated profile of the ideas of Confucius, but this summary of Confucianism should serve the student and journalist as a base for a philosophy. Many readers will undoubtedly find such a Confucian concept too regimented and socially determined and would believe that it would lead to a kind of robotized journalism devoid of personal satisfaction.

Such an obsession with individualism and freedom, of course, is part of the traditional Western philosophical perspective replete with its emphasis on personal achievement. What the Western journalist should recognize is that there are other ways of looking at journalism. Freedom may be of great importance to the Western journalist, but it is not as important to many Asian journalists as social concern, group loyalty, and harmonious human interaction. This is, at least, a main teaching of Confucius, one of history's great philosophical foundational mentors.

[2]

LAO-TZU

Lao-tzu, the traditional founder of Taoism in China, is an obscure figure of considerable philosophical stature. Exactly when he lived is not known, but his lifetime is usually considered to be from about 604 to 531 B.C. Some scholars doubt his very existence, and it may be that Chuang-tzu (c. 350–250 B.C.), a verified and great Taoist writer, is the real creator of the philosophy. If Lao-tzu did indeed live, we can say that his teachings were developed by his follower Chuang-tzu, and in much Chinese literature Taoism is called "Lao Chuang philosophy." Taoism is viewed as both a philosophy and religion, but it is as a philosophy that it has most to say to the modern American journalist.

Lao-tzu is thought to have been a native of Chu-jen (in today's Hunan Province), and his original name was Li Erh. He is said to have worked in the Imperial Court (perhaps in the Chou dynasty) as an archivist, dealing mainly with divination and astrology and sacred books; it was here that he became an outstanding *tzu* (intelligent or brilliant scholar). Some historical works mention his meeting with Confucius, but this is probably apocryphal.

The essential philosophical thought of Lao-tzu is found in the *Tao Te Ching,* believed by some to have been a handbook for rulers. *Tao* in Chinese originally meant "a road" or "a path." Lao-tzu said that one can find the *Tao* by following certain principles, after which we can live happily forever. But what exactly is the *Tao*? It cannot be told, but when it is found, one will know it.

One of the basic principles of Taoism is *wu-wei* (doing nothing to do everything)—a technique of achievement based on inaction. For example, force is never overcome by force but by a yielding. Lao-tzu taught that a person should do nothing for personal desire and that one should do nothing that violates the rules of nature. Such a passive philosophy would lead to happiness and social peace.

The Taoist journalist would be serene and have a subtle sense of humor. Such a journalist would be highly individualistic and, as Socrates also emphasized, would have self-knowledge and a respect for one's inner nature. Compassion would be a chief characteristic and would lead to a kind of journalism that would not have the Western aura of cold "objectivity." Not taking ambition and personal achievement seriously, the Taoist journalist would be concerned both with personal spiritual growth and insight and would feel that worldly possessions and success are not important. Such a journalist would have sympathy for the underdog, publicizing the misdeeds of the powerful and ridiculing arrogant, pompous, devious, and cruel people.

Confucianism, which sprang up in China at about the same time as Taoism, stresses a person's place in a group and is rather stern, regimented, and patriarchal, envisioning the poor, women, and children as needing authority and direction. Confucianism would appear to the Westerner to be more socially involved, "realistic," and collectivistic than Taoism, which is more sensitive, gentle, serene, and individualistic. Lao-tzu taught self-motivation and the acceptance of personal responsibility, characteristics that would seem to offset to some degree the childlikeness of his philosophy. The American Henry David Thoreau is a writer who was very much in tune with Taoist principles, especially in his emphasis on living peacefully—letting the waters of life flow around you.

Taoism stresses that a person is wrong to strive at achieving morality or "the good" as a goal. A personal campaign to do one's duty, believing that this is the way to be happy, is wrong for the Taoist. Both hedonism and utilitarianism are counterproductive; happiness and "the good" are not things to be obtained. Instead, they come to one through the right mental attitude; they cannot be sought out. When concepts such as good and evil are thought of as being objects to be attained or rejected, they lead to delusion and alienation. Lao-tzu presents this paradox: "When all the world recognizes good as good, it becomes evil." This means that this "good" becomes something desired and constantly pursued, leading to the frustration of striving after something that is unattainable.

The Taoist begins with the simple good that each person has by the fact of existence. Relieved of the self-consciousness of seeking the good, which we cannot grasp, we progress calmly through a simple life of humility—psychologically similar to the Christian "life of faith." So Lao-tzu would say: Don't try to seek out or accumulate virtue, but have it through non-action, which cares not for results or well-laid plans to achieve happiness. The Taoist's greatest happiness consists in doing nothing to seek happiness.

For Lao-tzu, the great person is one who is willing to wait, listen, and renounce useless striving. We should stop our attempts to understand through constant study—our trying to attain what cannot be attained. Then we will start to grow without knowing it; we will improve ourselves without any desire for self-improvement. We will never be happy as long as we attempt to be happy. This paradoxical teaching should not be misunderstood. Lao-tzu is not saying that we retreat from an active, human existence into a quietistic state; he is saying that happiness can be found, but only by non-seeking. If we accept and welcome everything—all that is being developed and being destroyed—without trying to mold and shape it to our own wishes, we will be happy because our joy comes from the freedom from striving.

Similar to the concepts of Alfred Korzybski and general semantics that would be introduced in the Western World centuries later, Lao-tzu taught that nothing is static and that everything is constantly undergoing mutations and change. In short, Taoism is a holistic philosophy, with everything merging and changing: beauty and ugliness, longness and shortness, highness and lowness, goodness and badness. This, too, is similar to general semantics, which stresses the relativity of concepts and the mutability of the entities of reality.

The world in all its aspects, including all life, is in flux, in a continual development. This is a central tenet of Taoism. Here we have an echo of a rough contemporary of Lao-tzu, the Greek philosopher Heraclitus. Everything is changing; what is good today may be bad tomorrow; what is ethical from one perspective may be unethical from another. The world, said Lao-tzu, is undefinable as well as constantly changing; and no matter how skillfully we use the language, we can never describe the world. The world is always greater than the sum of its parts; linguistic analysis always leaves something out. What we can convey by language is like seeing a leaf on a tree and believing that we are seeing the tree.

Lao-tzu would support governmental control of the press—that is, if the question arose. Such acceptance would conform with the principle of inaction; it would also protect the power of government from unwise criticism that might endanger its power. And, of course, it would protect the individual journalist from the trauma of being an adversary. Intervention by government, Taoism would postulate, would arouse enmity and friction that would threaten social harmony. Let things be; let the waters flow; permit natural activities to happen; cease all striving. This philosophy could also be applied to government: The best way for the government to control the press, according to Lao-tzu, would be to exercise no control.

Lao-tzu would say that every person should be allowed to speak freely so that information can move naturally to the rulers and be of value to the government. A good ruler should resemble the sea, perceived as powerful and generous. Such a sea is broad, having a lower position than the rivers and caring not where the rivers come from or what kinds of waters they carry. The good ruler is humble and permits every opinion to flow freely to him. The good ruler accepts criticism as well as compliments. This could likewise be said of the good journalist.

About the journalist Lao-tzu would probably add (paraphrasing what he did say about good soldiers and employers): A good journalist is not arrogant, violent, temperamental, vengeful, angry, or dominating. Rather, a good journalist is humble, peaceful, tolerant, and caring. A good journalist has much self-knowledge and self-respect, does not "make news" but, like a rock in a stream, permits the news to flow past. This passivity would, of course, be difficult for a modern journalist to understand or accept.

Lao-tzu is concerned about freedom of thought; if our mind is not free, we cannot find the truth. Journalists, he would say, too often have unfree minds that dictate stereotypical journalistic images and lead to mind-produced rather than reality-produced stories. We all live in a mental world as well as a real world, and journalists must be careful not to present the former rather than the latter.

Undoubtedly a Taoist journalist in the modern Western World would be a strange person, having no desires—even to report the truth. Why? Because only through having no desires could journalists find the truth. The Taoist journalist would look at the world as a whole and try to provide an image of it that would stress its interrelationships, not its discrete parts and events. Such a journalist would recognize that nothing is simply right or wrong, good or bad, beautiful or ugly, and that such antinomies can be applied to the same thing simultaneously, depending on the perspective held by the journalist. Every event would be simply an event to the Taoist journalist, not a good or bad event. Perhaps an impossible stance for the modern journalist? Certainly it would be an unusual one, calling on the journalist to give up the concepts of competition, striving, desiring, conspiring to "get ahead," and pursuing selfish ends. Lao-tzu would probably tell the journalist: Get ahead by staying behind; win by losing; and be happy by not chasing happiness.

[3]

SOCRATES

For the journalist who aspires to knowledge, understanding, serious thought, and self-understanding and who seeks answers to controversial questions, the Greek philosopher Socrates (469–399 B.C.) would most likely be a primary guide. Although Socrates himself left us nothing in writing, his ideas and influence have come to us through his student Plato and others who wrote of him (mainly Xenophon). He is generally considered the father of Western philosophy. Probably more than any of the world's great thinkers, Socrates stressed the importance of recognizing one's ignorance and persistently making a journey of thought, forever questioning, until one arrives at knowledge that is essential for a full and meaningful life. And for Socrates, education is that which people acquire for themselves—going beyond formal training—through continual thinking, probing, questioning, and conversing with serious and intelligent companions and acquaintances.

What a mission for today's journalist! Looking for answers: this is at the root of the Socratic method—a persistent and rigorous questioning (called the elenchus method) that pushes deeply into the hidden meaning of ideas and concepts. For Socrates this was not just an idle exercise, but one that forces members of a communication situation to seek a common understanding of the terms they use. Its hope of short-circuiting misunderstanding is certainly a worthy goal for the modern journalist.

Socrates lived in interesting times, growing up in powerful and prosperous Athens of Pericles after the Persian wars and reaching midlife during the disastrous Peloponnesian Wars. The earliest we hear of him is from Aristophanes in *The Clouds,* in which he is presented as a kind of clown. Much more light was shed on him by other Greek writers, especially by his student Plato in many of his writings. (It should be said, however, that it is impossible to know where Socrates' thought ends and Plato's takes up.) When Socrates was 70, the State accused him of impiety, of teaching young men idleness, corrupting the Athenian youth with strange ideas, and not believing in the country's gods. Tried and found guilty, he received a death sentence. But before the sentence could be executed, he drank hemlock and died in 399 B.C.

We do not know how Socrates supported himself during the years he talked with the eager youths of Athens. As far as we do know, he never worked or worried about tomorrow. He neglected his wife, Xanthippe, and children; although Xanthippe seemed to have loved him, she considered him an idler. Almost every social ideology—of that day and today—had its representative among those who flocked around Socrates to partake of his wisdom. Among them were Plato and Alcibiades, aristocrats; Aristippus, an anarchist; and Antisthenes, a socialist. His basic teachings were simple: Know thyself, he urged his students; realize that the only thing you know is that you know nothing; seek knowledge constantly, for only knowledge is virtue.

The journalist (or any person) interested in philosophy needs to become acquainted with Socrates through his dialogues, which provide a concrete encounter with direct and practical reason. Such an acquaintance will indicate the vital connections of ideas in the world, hard as most of them are to see. It will show the importance of using reason, understanding oneself, constantly seeking knowledge, and having a sense of humor. The starting point for living a moral life, for Socrates, is recognizing and understanding one's own prejudices, biases, and spiritual values. Only then can a person proceed to the important business of decreasing prejudices and increasing spiritual values.

In the dialogues or conversations that Socrates conducted

mainly with the Sophists (teachers of practical wisdom and oratory and arguers of any issue that Athenian citizens wished to bring up), he talked directly to individuals, forcing them to think, confusing them, insisting that they confront questions head-on and question conventional wisdom. The substance of such dialogues are to be found in Plato's depiction of talks with Socrates as he discussed ideas with such people as Meno, Thrasymachus, Cebes, Phaedrus, Laches, and Crito.

Socrates appeared to assume that troublesome terms had definitions. He felt that if these terms (for instance, courage, honor, justice, wisdom) could be discovered through systematic questioning, increased and important knowledge would result. Concept-clarification education: this might be the term for such a method in today's modern educational world. It is something that journalists need to be more concerned with, for too often labels and terms—such as liberal, progressive, patriotic, reactionary, terrorist—are thrown out to the public without a firm meaning attached to them.

What are the characteristics of the philosophical mood of Socrates, those that tend to define the person who is trying to philosophize? D. Elton Trueblood, a 20th-century American theologian and philosopher, has abstracted three of the most important (in his *General Philosophy,* 1963):

Skepticism. Socrates put doubt in the minds of the young men who heard him. For him, philosophy begins by raising catalytic questions, and he was a master at doing so. Be suspicious and critical of all judgments and generalizations, Socrates said. Such questioning should also be encased in an general aura of humor.

Catholicity. A provincialism of thought is a principal foe of philosophizing, for it hides much of the richness that contributes to the truth. Wisdom can be found in a great variety of ideas, historical periods, cultures, and personal philosophies. Idealists can learn from realists, liberals from conservatives, scientists from artists, and vice versa, of course. Socrates would advise taking from many places what is reasonable, intellectually stimulating, and useful in the accumulation of knowledge and wisdom.

Practicality. Philosophy, Socrates believed, must make a practical difference in one's life. The end of philosophizing is using ideas to reach sound conclusions that can make a difference in the real world of living. Theory and practice must be harmonious in one's life, theory serving as a guide to action. According to Socrates, when one seeks knowledge or truth, it should be for a practical purpose: to make for a more virtuous and happy life.

At the core of Socratic teaching was this concern for virtuous living. Socrates had his own religious faith, believing in one God and some kind of immortality. But he wanted a moral code that would transcend religion. We all seek our own good, Socrates said, but it is easy to mistake just what that is. So we must diligently search for what constitutes this good. And if we find it? This leads to one of Socrates' most controversial ideas—that if a person *knows* "the good," that person will *do* good. When we at last know what is good, and that is not easy, then it is impossible for us to do evil. According to Socrates, knowledge is virtue, and nobody knowingly does evil. Ever since this premise surfaced in Plato's dialogues, philosophers have debated its validity and ramifications. We might ask: If the journalist knows the right thing to do, will he or she actually do it? That is the question—and a very important one.

In a dialogue with Thrasymachus recorded in Plato's *Republic,* Socrates questions him about might making right. Thrasymachus believes that might is "the good" and therefore leads one to doing the right thing. Socrates leads Thrasymachus (or the listener to the dialogue) to the conclusion that might is not the good and that it leads to wrong actions, not right ones. Socrates is not saying that might is not workable in the practical world or that it does not succeed in accomplishing certain ends; the truth he is unfolding is that might should not, in a moral sense, be equated with "the right."

This idea of power and its relationship to ends and means,

developed more fully by Machiavelli in the 16th century, has definite implications for today's journalist. How does the journalist use power? Do perceived worthy ends demand unworthy means? Is it "right" for the journalist to use journalistic "might"—for instance, invading privacy or using misleading techniques—to get a story?

If Socrates were among us today, he would undoubtedly ask journalists many definitional questions, not the least of which might be: What is journalism? Or, what is news? Or, what is "a right to know"? Or, what is objectivity in newswriting? Some of the most basic terms in journalism continue to be virtually undefined. And today, as when Socrates was questioning the Sophists in the streets of Athens, fuzzy concepts lead to ambiguity and confusion about the foundational philosophy of journalism. Before we can come to any grand conclusions about journalistic ethics or purpose, Socrates would tell us, we must be able to define and understand our basic concepts.

Socrates obviously enjoyed his "dialectic" game of deflating dogmas, refining definitions, puncturing old assumptions, and playing the gadfly. It is a game played daily in the modern arena of journalism, and the intellectually awake journalist, the one who desires to plunge into the swirling waters of contemporary controversy and debate, will revel in following the Socratic path.

[4]

PLATO

The Greek philosopher Plato (427–347 B.C.) was born into an aristocratic family at a time of great turmoil in the city-state of Athens. War with Sparta was going on, and Athens was in the midst of much political, social, and moral conflict. It was during this turbulent period that Plato's teacher, Socrates, was imprisoned and died by drinking hemlock. At that time Plato was about 30. After traveling to Egypt and Sicily, he returned to Athens and founded his famous school, the Academy, which had many illustrious Greek thinkers as students—Aristotle among them.

Plato's own philosophy develops Socratic themes, especially those defining such concepts as justice and courage. Probably his most prominent theory about the nature of reality is his famous Theory of Ideas (or Forms), in which he sees a realm of perfect eternal Forms that lies, unchanging, behind the dynamic world of material objects. This concept of Ideas gave rise to his being considered a progenitor of what is called idealism. Only by the intellect, says Plato, can these Ideas or Forms be known.

The Republic is Plato's most famous work; it is a dialogue in which Socrates and others talk about justice and its relationship to the perfect state and the characteristics needed by citizens and rulers in such a state. The modern journalist desiring insights into virtue, justice, political theory, and motivations for political activity will find *The Republic* "must reading." For example, in several dialogues one can find the fascinating conversations with the Sophist Thrasymachus, who argues that power is preferable to virtue and, in so doing, anticipates the 16th-century Machiavelli and all journalists who justify almost any reportorial means by desired ends.

Another relevant part of Plato's thought for journalists is his well-known allegory of the Cave in *The Republic* (Book VII) in which he depicts prisoners, chained with their backs to the cave entrance, the one opening of light. A fire burns on the open slope leading from the cave's entrance, reflecting the shadows of passing people onto the cave wall in front of the prisoners. These prisoners, Plato has Socrates say, have never seen the real world outside; they only experience the shadows of people and their voices. They therefore consider the shadows and echoes to be reality; it is the only reality they have. Socrates asks his listeners to suppose that one prisoner is released and taken into the sunlight outside the cave. Now he can see reality as it is, not merely as shadows and echoes indicate.

Journalists can be seen as providing their audiences with mere shadows on the wall; what they provide as fact or truth is nothing more than flickering shadows, distortions of reality. Perhaps the best recent book to delve into this allegory is by philosopher Jay Newman—*The Journalist in Plato's Cave* (1989).

Plato is arguably the father of Western collectivism or statism, and the ideas for such flow from his philosophy of idealism. This metaphysics posits that the universe is made up of two contrary dimensions: true reality (a supernatural, perfect, non-material realm) and the material world in which we live. This material world, like the shadows on the cave wall, is only a distorted and false reflection of reality. For Plato, reality is basically spiritual or non-material—simply an Idea—and this forms the basics of Plato's idealism.

What this means is that individual people are not real but are actually the same one Form or Idea in many manifestations; therefore, people are not autonomous. Thus, Plato sees people gathered in society as the main standard of value, the "community as a whole," with each person wiping out his or her individuality and merging into the aggregate or collective.

The omnipotent State follows naturally. The authority of the State, says Plato, must be unlimited. Government-approved ideas must be stamped on the people; State-run schools would educate everyone; government would censor all literature and art, assign all people to their vocations, and regulate their economic activities. In both Plato's *Republic* and the *Laws,* one can find the details of this blueprint for the totalitarian ideal state.

This collectivistic philosophy of Plato, if applied to journalism, would lead to individualism being largely sacrificed on the altar of collective or institutional progress (defined by the executives) and harmony (meaning no internal friction). The individual journalist who wants to have a voice in the policy of a newspaper, for instance, or who considers institutional friction as beneficial, would bc lost in Plato's newspaper. Many modern journalists, regardless of what they might wish for, perhaps would admit that mass media do subscribe to this Platonic collectivism, with the editors virtually determining everything and the functionaries (the journalists) having little or no power.

The Platonic communitarian spirit does not reflect the spirit of individualism, soon after Plato to be championed by Aristotle and his individualistic followers in more recent times. The existentialists, for example, would find this system of Plato's most distressing and would see in it a "death wish" for individual personal autonomy. Aristotle was soon to deny Plato's concept of Forms, maintaining that there is only one reality—the world of particulars. According to Aristotle, the individual should not be submerged in society but held high in his or her particularity and prized.

Plato would have left morality in the hands of his "philosopher kings." Such intellectual rulers in *The Republic* formulated good laws, ideal laws, the best possible laws, for the State's governance. The citizen was automatically led in the direction of the good, the ethical, and the just. Ignorant themselves of the nature of virtue, citizens attained true virtue simply by abiding by the State's laws. So in a Platonic state the ethics of the people were derived not from personal understanding and reason but from following public opinion and the laws.

In effect, the ordinary citizen's morality is always conventional, says Plato. Such a citizen is too busy, or too ignorant, to discover and solve moral dilemmas. So for Plato the citizen's sense of right and wrong would come from without, by the collective pressure of public opinion led by public education. Plato put his finger on what he called the "paradox of freedom" in his criticism of democracy, noting that a free people could freely determine to become enslaved. This would be unfortunate, says Plato, because quite probably they would choose an unqualified person as their tyrant, not a public-spirited, qualified philosopher king.

In short, Plato's ethics would be strictly utilitarian—a kind of Statist Utilitarianism, in which the criterion for morality is the interest of the State. Whatever furthers this interest, says Plato, is "good and virtuous and just," and whatever threatens it is bad, wicked, and unjust. Plato is advocating a kind of aristocracy of the best, the wisest, and most socially minded of them all—the philosopher kings. Here we would have the State defining morality, and by projection to journalism, we would have publishers and editors defining media ethics.

Despite Plato's ethical utilitarianism (for the State), he did have some rather definite ideas relating to the nature of a virtuous person. Certainly modern journalists would find his cardinal virtues, discussed in *The Republic,* of help (in spite of considerable semantic noise surrounding them). First, Plato mentions *wisdom,* which gives direction to the moral life and is the intellectual base for ethics. Wisdom comes largely from maturing, from contemplation, reading, conversing, and study. Next is *courage,* which keeps one pursuing goals that wisdom has set. The third virtue is *temperance,* which urges moderation or the blending of intuition, thought, and other human tendencies. This virtue gives harmony to the moral life and keeps one away from fanaticism. And finally there is *justice,* which involves considering a person's "deservedness." This does not mean, for Plato, that each person has to be treated like every other. For example, justice would not require that all public officials receive equal attention on television or the same amount of newspaper space. Justice must satisfy "deservedness" and does not mean equal treatment.

Of course, the journalist knows clearly that the main problem here is determining just who deserves special treatment.

Although Plato has some pessimistic things to say to the journalist in the area of epistemology—such as the necessity of abstracting from reality and the impossibility of presenting a realistic version of an event—he does provide an incentive for the journalist to work harder to approach the light at the entrance to the darkened cave. But Plato gives little encouragement to the journalist who wants maximum freedom. For Plato sees freedom as freedom to help society (or one of its instrumentalities) achieve what is required for the social good.

The Platonists put the social good above the concept of freedom. Likewise, they would surely place press responsibility above the concept of press freedom. This would entail a kind of "positive freedom" for the press—the freedom to do something positive for society. Such a concept has a great appeal for many journalists and commentators (such as the well-known Hutchins Commission of the mid-1940s), people imbued with a liberalism and social concern inherited from Plato. But it does not sit well with many journalists who see such a philosophy as endangering their freedom and autonomy. Such people are more comfortable with Aristotle.

Probably no philosopher has matched Plato in the effect he has had on Western Civilization—in its thinking, social life, or politics. Plato's complexity permits various interpretations of his stimulating ideas, many of them probably quite different from the ones presented here. It has been said that all philosophy is merely a footnote to Plato. Whether this is true or not, there is no doubt that a journalist who reads him will come away a wiser person. This brief profile, of course, is only a shadow on Plato's wall, giving no more than a flickering image of perhaps history's greatest thinker.

[5]

ARISTOTLE

The journalist wanting to take the correct action, do the right thing, and live up to the best morality will certainly want to consider the foundational principles of one of history's greatest philosophers, Aristotle (384–322 B.C.). Not only a brilliant philosopher, this most famous of Plato's students was also a scientist and logician of note. Here is a down-to-earth philosopher who emphasizes the positive and develops a full vision of a virtuous and happy person, stressing full personal development, an appreciation of self-worth, and personal happiness and progress.

He also would tell the journalist of today to be suspicious of an egalitarian and collectivistic society. In morality, likewise, he would prize individual virtue above all and would enthrone self-esteem and self-development. And certainly he would say that happiness or intellectual pleasure (*eudaemonia*) is a composite of such things as wisdom, excellence, friendship, moderation, reason, and contemplation—all things that help us to live and fare well. All the while, he would remind the journalist that a life of moderation in all things is needed for a happy and virtuous existence.

Aristotle founded his school, called the Lyceum, near Athens, and some of his lectures there served as the basis for what came to be a great treatise called *The Nicomachean Ethics,* named possibly for Aristotle's son, Nicomachus, although scholars are uncertain about the origin of the book's title. In Book 1 of this work, Aristotle discusses the characteristics of *eudaemonia* and later presents his famous concept of the Golden Mean, showing great concern for proper balance and moderation. Basically he says that ethical or right behavior is the balance or mean between doing injustice and having injustice done to you.

Recognizing the difficulty in finding this ethical mean, Aristotle tries to shed some light on the subject by this explication: moral excellence is a mean between two kinds of badness—one of excess and the other of defect; virtue is hard to achieve because it is not easy to find the middle point; it is easy to be extreme in language, thought, and action, but to be moderate (to the right extent, at the right time, with the right object, and in the right way) is not easy. And, Aristotle admits, with great understatement, not everyone can achieve this Golden Mean.

The journalist trying to find the Aristotelian mean is left alone to search for it in every specific situation. The journalist must decide where the balance lies; it is a personal decision to be wrestled with and determined by the individual person. Many will consider this ethical mean vague, and it is. Aristotle offers a challenge that is much like that presented by the modern existentialist who puts responsibility directly in the hands of each person; that person must make the determination and accept the consequences.

Aristotle would advise journalists to decide which extreme poses the most danger to them and to stay away from that extreme, and while doing this, to avoid going too far toward the other extreme. If a journalist knows that he or she is prone to sensationalize, to overplay, in a story, that journalist must determine to stay away from that extreme and write with caution and moderation, even to the point of being a little dull. The mean, then, in an ethical sense, may not be the exact midway point, but slightly on the "safe" side of the mean.

Although Aristotle seems to be flexible in his ethics, it would be a mistake to see him as a "situation" ethicist. He classifies some actions and thoughts as absolutely bad and never even relatively desirable: actions such as murder, adultery, and theft and feelings such as shamelessness, envy, and malice. No Golden Mean here; these are evil and unethical in themselves, and the moral person should avoid them. But Aristotle is no

Kant, who was not open to compromise and moderation. He is more relativistic and hinges his ethics, in most situations, on seeking the Golden Mean.

A common journalistic ethical quandary is determining how far to go in telling the truth. The journalist may ask himself or herself, Should I report all the truth I know and have verified (one extreme), or should I take liberties with the truth for some personal or altruistic reason (the other extreme)? The journalist is left with the responsibility of determining the proper middle approach; there is no rule book for this. It is a personal decision, to be made in every particular case.

Some of the extremes constantly facing the journalist and needing reconciliation with the Golden Mean are these: excessive/skimpy description; invading privacy/overcautious observing and questioning; insensitive pictures of an accident victim/avoidance of realism in pictures; overzealous accuracy in quotes/frequent and liberal tampering with quotes. For Aristotle in such cases, it is not an "either/or" situation; rather, it is seeking the proper balance, the correct moderation.

Aristotle had great respect for the individual and championed self-respect and self-aggrandizement. The good life, for Aristotle, is one of personal self-fulfillment, of enjoying the values of the world. Every person should work to achieve happiness, to grow in character. Aristotle believes that we are not born with "character"; we must build it as we go along. Character depends on the kind of nurturing we have, and we also develop character, he says, by practice and repetition. Finally it becomes habitual, effortless, and second nature. Proper moral training, however, is not coercive; it is freely taught and freely learned.

A rational pride in oneself and one's moral character, when it is deserving, is the highest of all virtues, according to Aristotle. Such a virtuous person relies on intelligence as a guide, loving and indulging this rational aspect of self, and is "to the fullest extent a lover of himself." Therefore, says Aristotle, it is right for the good person to be self-loving. Why is this? Because that person will benefit from doing good actions, and at the same time that person will be helpful to others.

This sounds somewhat like the 20th century's Ayn Rand, who considered herself an Aristotelian. However, where Rand scorns sacrificial altruism, Aristotle sees the good person as willing to sacrifice all the prizes of life—even, if need be, life itself—to play a noble part. However, it can be said that Aristotle differed from his mentor Plato, who saw the good life chiefly as one of selflessness, of renouncing the pleasures of this world for those of a more intellectual level. Plato would negate his own individuality also in order to become a cooperating part of the society or collective.

Aristotle also denies the mystical elements of Plato's philosophy and proposes reason, rather than intuition, as a way to achieve knowledge. He is a proponent of objectivity and concentrates on the reality and concreteness of specific entities in the world; he turns away from the relativism, subjectivity, and epistemological idealism of Plato.

No democrat, Aristotle believed in an aristocratic political philosophy and morality. He was a conservative, seeing the turmoil that had come from Athenian democracy; he longed for order, security, and peace. He distrusted the communitarian efficiency and power of society as formulated by Plato, seeing in it a devaluing of the individual, privacy, and liberty. Representing the aristocrat in morality, Aristotle also would have his ideal person equipped with all human excellences—of character, intellect, health, looks, and birth. Such a person of character would act appropriately to the situation, and this must be determined by reason. Of course, people of character in the Aristotelian sense would reason as he did, thus keeping this situation-acting from falling into a pluralistic and meaningless relativism.

The modern journalist who respects individualism, reason, the scientific approach, objectivity, absolutes, self-fulfillment, and personal happiness will find a friend in Aristotle. No mysticism (found in Plato and later the German idealists and romantics) for Aristotle, no skepticism, no limitations on the human spirit or human accomplishments.

Habit was very important to Aristotle, as it was for Confucius. One develops virtue through habit; acting virtuously should be second nature, said Aristotle, who saw the virtuous act performed as if by instinct, with a person making no moral effort each time it is repeated. He refers to moral goodness as "the child of habit," noting that its very name—ethics—is derived from *ethos* (distinctive spirit or character). We learn virtues and develop them through habit; moral virtues, believed Aristotle, are not implanted in us by Nature. In a sense Aristotle is saying that what determines a person's excellent character is not merely what he or she does but what he or she *likes* doing.

The journalist may on occasion do something not befitting his or her character (for example, playing too loosely with a source's quotes), but the action will cause discomfort and pain. Nevertheless, that journalist is still a person of character, having deviated from habitual practices only temporarily. So character depends not so much on what the journalist does from time to time but on what he or she feels comfortable doing and has habitual enjoyment in doing. Aristotle, then, would emphasize character rather than moral virtue—having a person acting effortlessly in a correct way rather than constantly needing to indulge in moral reasoning as the circumstances come up.

How do we know whether we are acting virtuously? If we feel pleasure in our actions, says Aristotle, we are acting virtuously, for it is with pleasure and pain that virtue is concerned. For Aristotle the moral end is happiness. He defined virtue as a habit of choice, the characteristic of reaching moderation in action determined by reason or as the "prudent man" would conceive it. Aristotle would tell today's journalist that who he or she *is* is more important than what he or she *does* in specific cases. Emphasizing the positive, Aristotle would tell the journalist that what is important is *essence of life,* in habitually being a virtuous person regardless of negative lapses. This is the secret of morality, rather than following strict codes of conduct.

The virtuous person, in Aristotle's view, does have some

definite characteristics. Going beyond his strong belief in *meden agan* (nothing in excess), here are 10 prime definers of Aristotle's "ethical Superman" selected from his *Ethics*. Such a person (1) keeps out of needless danger and confrontation, (2) has a disposition of service to others, (3) does not take part in public displays, (4) talks and acts frankly and authentically, (5) never feels malice and forgets and passes over injuries, (6) does not want to be praised or to blame others, (7) speaks no evil of others, even enemies, (8) is not prone to vehemence, for he considers nothing very important, (9) bears life's trials and tribulations with dignity and grace, and (10) is his own best friend and delights in privacy.

This Aristotelian concept of virtue encapsulates and forecasts the principal traits of the moral and happy person extolled by almost all the moral philosophers and religious teachers who followed him. The modern journalist would do well to take the ideas of Aristotle seriously even if it is not always easy to be enthusiastic about the person Aristotle. Unlike Plato, Aristotle was not very enthusiastic about anything, his motto being *nil admirari*—admire or marvel at nothing. It is much easier to admire Plato, with his social consciousness and reforming zeal. But perhaps it is good for the world to have had the calm rationalism and individualism of Aristotle to balance the more flamboyant idealism and collectivism of Plato.

[6]

NICCOLÒ MACHIAVELLI

One of the forerunners of political science, Niccolò Machiavelli (1469–1527) was an Italian political philosopher, historian, poet, and playwright born in Florence. He was first to develop the idea that political leaders are not bound by conventional morality and to insist that power and its cunning use is of utmost importance. His life was divided between an active political period and a time of retirement when he did most of his writing. All of his important books were written after 1512 when he was relieved of his governmental functions in Florence.

Machiavelli presented a philosophy that might well presage the development of a pragmatic, success-oriented, hard-nosed journalism. His advice to rulers of the late 15th- and early 16th-century Italian city-states can easily be related to journalism of the 20th century. Machiavelli's name has become associated with a certain kind of behavior (called Machiavellianism) marked by acting out of expediency, ignoring normal moral rules and conscience, and exhibiting a kind of devilish cunning and pragmatic virtuosity (*virtù*).

Machiavelli was a devotee of power and its sly and manipulative use. And modern journalism, wherever it is found, is considered an instrument for social development, a necessary agenda-setter or agent of control. It follows that many people who control the press wield great social influence. Journalism's power is used in different ways in different social systems, but the common journalistic question almost everywhere is this: How can we achieve our ends?

Machiavellians certainly can be found in American journalism. The practical, success-oriented, competitive, and power-hungry press—at least large portions of it—has found the foundations set by Machiavelli extremely useful. The highly egoistic, individualistic, competitive philosophy inspired by the European Enlightenment found Machiavellianism a compatible foundation.

Along with the strong positive strain of idealistic, altruistic public concern apparent in journalism today, we can also see a deep current of exploitative journalism that mainly benefits journalists, not the public. Some American journalists, in vigorously seeking objectives and achieving ends, evidence Machiavellian tendencies. Although normally Machiavelli is associated with egocentric concerns, such an image is perhaps unfair. Even the most socially conscious, altruistic editor can use Machiavellian tactics. It is not just the firmness and determination, the skill and courage with which the journalist seeks success, but also the lengths to which he or she will go and the tactics used that determine Machiavellianism in the press.

In *The Prince* (1513) and *Discourses* (1513–17) Machiavelli had much to say about the tactics of power and success that many journalists have used to great advantage. Walter Lippmann has said that Machiavelli is one of the most reviled men in history but probably has the greatest number of followers.

It should be remembered, however, that Machiavelli assumed that the prince personifies the good of the State, and the good of the State is predicated on the overriding aim of the State to persist and be powerful. Therefore, for Machiavelli, the State's existence and power were ends in themselves. All other considerations must be sacrificed to these ends. It may be straining, but it might be said that one could look at journalism (or a mass medium) in the same way: it must continue to exist and must enhance its power.

Machiavelli was a political person and historian. He was also an ethicist—of a very pragmatic type; in fact, many philosophers would consider him a proponent of amorality, or a kind of expediency ethics. He was the first political (read: journalistic) thinker to develop the idea that morality differs from and is not bounded by the usual ethical norms. He also introduced the important concept that power is the decisive factor in political (read: journalistic) life.

Machiavellian journalism would be goal-oriented; it would be rather abrasive, even arrogant. In ethics—if Machiavelli can be thought of as ethical at all—he had an overriding maxim that seemed to combine both duty and consequences: "Do those things that will maximize personal success." He would bind today's journalists to such a deontological principle, one that is obviously egoistic. This is not the course for the altruistic journalist, but nobody has contended that Machiavelli was an altruist.

By all means succeed, Machiavelli would tell the modern journalist. And also, by *any* means. Achieve your objective, he would say. Get that story. Of course, if getting the story goes against your goal of "ends," then do not get it. Or it is possible that Machiavelli would advise the journalist to get only those parts of the story consistent with the overall purpose. So actually he would see journalistic tactics as effective or ineffective, not as ethical or unethical.

Machiavelli would want the journalist to be a virtuoso, a person relying on what he called *virtù*—decisiveness and ingenuity. Journalists should be determined, persistent, and risk-taking. Or as he said in *The Prince,* they need to be strong as lions and cunning as foxes. However, this journalistic virtuosity, indicating our freedom and stemming from strength and cunning, is greatly impaired. Freedom, for Machiavelli, is always restricted by Fortune (*fortuna*), or chance, which determines so much of what happens to us; so for the journalist, there is no need to expect to act freely any more than half the time. But even if we forcefully use our virtuosity only half the time, according to Machiavelli, we can accomplish much and satisfy most of our desires.

In line with Machiavelli's ideas, the journalist would not

seek love, but respect. And this would come through the exercise of power. Journalism's main mission, he would say, is to wield power, to influence society, to shape and help determine government. Journalism is a self-defined, egocentric institution that leads and does not follow—except on occasion when it is expedient to do so. Its mission is to protect itself, to grow, and to use power for its own ends. It is motivated by self-interest and egoism, although it creates the illusion of altruism. Machiavellian journalism would be obsessed by its own freedom but would make a great pretense of social responsibility.

The mission of a journalism steeped in Machiavellian philosophy would be to solidify its own power by dulling the intellect of the citizens, by offering them mainly intellectual desserts, by luring them into playful hours, by causing them to feel rather than think, and by providing them with bits and pieces of reality so that they will know a world of only discontinuity and stereotypes. It would not be a mission designed to make more discerning and sophisticated citizens.

Such a journalistic concept sets out to create a world of images for the people—a world that feeds upon itself, that stimulates further stimulation, further abstraction, further and simpler distortions. The ultimate goal of such Machiavellianism would be the ushering of vast audiences into a media world that is unreal but seems real. Machiavelli would feel that journalism should define and structure the world for the people, giving them a certain comfort in the face of a frightening and all-encompassing environment.

Machiavellian journalism would be safe from public harm because of basic and general public ignorance. How can the people mistrust the press when they know almost nothing except what the press tells them? If anything, Machiavelli would say, the press fails to use the power it has, with many journalists going through their days functioning as mere robots, uttering shibboleths about their Constitutional freedoms but showing no enterprise and courage, showing no inclination to use the great power they have. The Machiavellian journalist would use power regularly, not fritter it away in the daily tedium of unsystematized activity.

Machiavelli would see his kind of press as valuing its own freedom. With freedom, it can expand power. However, freedom is bad if it causes a social or state reaction that endangers or narrows press power. Freedom unused or chaotically used is either valueless or anarchic, Machiavelli would say, being himself a proponent of discipline and social direction and opposed to a dormant or aimless use of freedom.

One aspect of freedom, for the Machiavellian, is the freedom to determine tactics for success. The Machiavellian would definitely make use of any means necessary to achieve a desired end, in line with Machiavelli's great respect for power and success. As to responsible journalism, Machiavelli would say that a journalist is acting responsibly when he or she achieves the desired end. A newspaper or TV station is responsible when it gets the story. Journalism's responsibility is to succeed: that is the Machiavellian philosophy.

As to public-service journalism, Machiavellian journalism would do what is good for the journalist and the press institution. A guiding principle would be: Help others if it helps you. Be kind to others if being kind augments your image or helps you achieve your purposes. But do not waste valuable time on others if nothing positive for you is likely to result. This note is important: Machiavelli stressed the fact that he was not giving a blueprint for honorable behavior or how society should be run; rather, he was simply dealing with the question of how society *is* run and how people *do* behave and therefore how a ruler must behave if he wishes to survive.

Finally, let us look briefly at how Machiavelli's ideas impinge on journalistic ethics. Machiavelli would give little thought to what we normally think of as press ethics. He was a believer in expediency, in pragmatics. If anything, Machiavelli would probably be a consequentialist—one who acts with consequences in mind. Machiavellian journalists would not be consequentialists like John Stuart Mill, thinking of maximizing the happiness of others; rather, they would think of the consequences to themselves. They would believe in egoistic consequentialism.

Machiavelli would think that journalists often harm themselves, confuse and frustrate themselves, by worrying about the ethics of their actions. A concern for ethics is dangerous to a good journalist because such concern makes the journalist timid, even cowardly, and replaces firm decision with indecision. Use normal ethical rules or expectations when you can, Machiavelli would say, but when they won't work, use any means that will. Journalists of the Machiavellian stripe would not want to alienate people unnecessarily, but when they anticipated failure from abiding by social norms, they would bend—or ignore—the usual rules and expectations.

It is obvious that Machiavellian journalism differs significantly from a journalism informed by Christian principles. The Christian journalist would be an altruist, not an egoist, and would focus on the transcendent "beyond," largely turning away from worldly affairs (being *in* the world but not *of* it) and thereby discouraging the development of Machiavellian virtuosity. Such an overriding concern for spiritual matters and the welfare of others, Machiavelli would say, would be the main cause of journalistic weakness and the inability to achieve success. The Machiavellian journalist would see religion as a way of depreciating one's self-image and self-worth, of being a form of self-sacrifice, and of causing altruism to rule personal actions. As this point of view would place others higher than personal success, it would make the journalist virtually impotent. Therefore, the Machiavellian would see a Christian journalism, if practiced, as bringing an end to success-oriented journalism.

Machiavellian journalism is certainly not for everybody, but it is probably more popular than it appears to be. Although altruistic philosophy connected closely with consequential considerations overtly governs American journalism, beneath the surface can be found a sizable egoistic and pragmatic driving force that smacks strongly of Machiavellianism.

[7]

MICHEL DE MONTAIGNE

Probably history's pre-eminent personal essayist, Michel de Montaigne (1533–1592) was a French thinker and writer who was able to express universal ideas and thoughts that traversed centuries because he took seriously the ancient Greek admonition "Know Thyself." He believed that in knowing oneself, a person could gain insights into all of humanity. This deep-rooted belief of Montaigne's resulted in one of the world's great books, his celebrated *Essays,* some 107 of them running to more than 1,000 pages.

At least one type of journalist today, the personal columnist and even the editorial writer, can learn much from Montaigne. Such a writer can, by honest, forthright, personal writing, open vistas for the reader that are beyond the reach of more impersonal, formal, and "objective" journalists. Montaigne invented the personal essay, creating a flexible genre that was at the same time controlled, loose, elastic, digressive, and familiar. Such a form, if used by imaginative, insightful journalists, can make the most mundane and humble personal incidents and descriptions into universal truths that highlight the human story.

Montaigne would advise journalists, even hard-nosed investigative reporters, to look deep within themselves and try to understand their values, biases, and basic philosophical and religious underpinnings. He would say that such introspection will help them provide a personal dimension to their journalism that will give it a universal element of credibility and humanism. If journalists do not know themselves, Montaigne would say, there is little likelihood that they will be able to know much about anyone else.

Montaigne believed that honesty is essential for one to

receive larger truths from self-examination. We must cut through natural barriers, such as vanity, bias, and self-deceit, and look directly at the "real us," the flawed but always interesting selves that hide beneath the surface of our image. Montaigne would dispute the "scientist" who insists that a person cannot project his or her own thoughts, ideas, opinions, and feelings onto other people. If honestly viewed, Montaigne would say, self-projection to others and to all of humankind will shed much light on the human condition.

Another useful piece of advice from Montaigne for the journalist: Eschew abstractness in your writing. Have a direct style that is at once playful, metaphoric, image-laden, humble, light, and commonsensical. But don't let your style dominate to the point of obscuring content, because content should always be the most important part of writing. Style and content, for Montaigne, would live comfortably together and provide pleasure and insight for the reader.

Humor is another important facet of writing for Montaigne. Laugh at yourself, and then you can laugh at others. Have a sense of humor in writing that never deprives others of their sense of worth or dignity. Often, ideas can be presented much more effectively through a light and humorous touch, with the frequent use of personal anecdote, than through a serious rhetorical style. One of Montaigne's heroes was Socrates, a person revered for his honesty, naturalness, and sense of humor.

What Montaigne exemplifies most, and what he would recommend to the journalistic editorial writer, is candor, honesty, clarity, humor, and persistence. He would advise journalists not only to write about themselves but to *be* themselves. Who a person is comes out in that person's writing; what a person writes about himself or herself then becomes a part of who that person becomes. There is an existential ring to this, and in this respect Montaigne certainly shares an affinity with those existentialists (such as Kierkegaard, Nietzsche, and Sartre) who came along later.

Montaigne put little faith in empiricism, feeling that the senses cannot be depended upon, that they deceive the intellect. He would rather be guided by personal observations, insights, and results than by reason. Logic, he thought, had laughable limitations. And rationalism did not appeal to him because he doubted that universal truth could be found through reason. For Montaigne, that could be accomplished only through a religion based on self-examination and understanding. Many commentators on Montaigne, however, have noted that his *Essays* is a good example of using the rational process to degrade the principle of reason.

Like any good essayist (and he is probably history's greatest), Montaigne does not preach; he teaches through showing, through piling up personal anecdotes to illustrate points, through probing deeply into life's little matters, following the modern journalistic maxim of "Show, don't tell" that journalists and journalism students of today recognize. Montaigne is not self-righteous; he is modest; he is humble; he is honest; and in his self-revelatory writing he reveals something important about all of us.

In journalism Montaigne would consider even the small, seemingly inconsequential events worth considering. Nothing that happens to a person is too unimportant to think about. He disliked fanatics or those who gravitate to extremes, but he felt that knowing about such extremists was helpful to self-knowledge. He also had little use for artificialities; for him, life was too short to lose valuable time dealing with vacuous, time-wasting trifles.

Universities of his day, and certainly also of ours, gave little attention to morality, and this saddened Montaigne. He thought that a moral educational foundation was essential, and the universities (which he called "yap shops") made little or no contribution to this foundation. One wonders what he would think of television and its "greatest titillation principle" today, but one can imagine.

Montaigne believed in developing an ethical system

through rigorous introspection. Nobody can be taught morality, he believed; perhaps all that can be done is to teach what it is about. Morality comes from within, wells up from introspection and concern, and impinges on both the self-development of each person and the beneficial harmony and progress of society. Perhaps as much as anyone, Montaigne came closest to living the Golden Mean of Aristotle, saying that "greatness of soul" is not found by striving upward but by finding one's place within a moderate position rather than an extreme one. "Nothing," he wrote, "is so beautiful, so right, as acting as a man should nor is any learning so arduous as knowing how to live this life naturally and well."

Journalists today can learn much from Montaigne, not only about the craft of writing but about how to live a good life. Montaigne's skepticism, his love of the adventure of life, his capacity to learn about others by learning about himself, and his unremitting honesty tinged with humor and self-criticism all combined to make this French thinker a worthy teacher for the journalist.

[8]

JOHN MILTON

One of the big names in American journalism is the British poet and writer John Milton (1608–1674). When the subject of freedom of expression comes up, Milton's name always emerges, along with his famous indictment of censorship, *Areopagitica,* published in 1644. American journalists consider Milton a foundational hero, a thinker who was the first to plant the idea of a free press firmly in the intellectual soil of England, where it was later transferred to the American Colonies.

Milton's strong assault on censorship, unlike his pamphlets in favor of divorce, caused little concern among governmental and religious authorities when it was published. For nearly a century the pamphlet served as no real catalyst for free expression; it was not until 1735 (during the trial of John Peter Zenger in America) that *Areopagitica* ignited a wave of demands for free expression and an end to censorship.

Censorship was well established in England when the tract was first published. The situation worsened throughout the first half of the 17th century, and many pamphleteers were brought before the infamous Star Chamber and imprisoned and punished severely. At one point in these turbulent times, Milton was arrested and other Protestant followers of Oliver Cromwell were killed. Milton saw censorship at the time as a product of the Catholic Inquisition; therefore, it should be scorned as something alien to what he considered to be a Protestant England.

Throughout Milton's long life he was an ardent Puritan and questioned Christian orthodoxy. He was a devoted biblical scholar, and his interest in religion led to his great epic poem *Paradise Lost* (1667). His opposition to the Church of England

and Catholicism was constant and often bitter; in fact, after Milton became Latin Secretary to the Council of State (in the Cromwell Protectorate) in 1649, for two decades he censored Catholic writings and condemned Catholics as "papist rabble and savages." This sojourn into the world of censorship and hatred for those he opposed cast a dark shadow on his earlier avowed love for reason and free expression.

Nevertheless, history has tended to forget or overlook this contradiction in Milton's life and to keep him perched high at the pinnacle of free expression. Especially admired by journalists is Milton's idea that truth will emerge victorious over falsehood in what was more recently termed the "marketplace of ideas" by Oliver Wendell Holmes; today, this "victory" is called "the self-righting principle." Milton's famous passage from *Areopagitica* expresses this concept well: "And though all the winds of doctrine were let loose to play upon the earth, so Truth be in the field, we do injuriously, by licensing and prohibiting, to misdoubt her strength. Let her and Falsehood grapple; whoever knew Truth put to the worse, in a free and open encounter?"

As stirring and noble as these words are, they do not describe the real Milton, whose strong Protestantism never permitted him to tolerate Roman Catholicism. Not really democratic in his concept of freedom of expression, he believed in censorship for the masses, which he considered a "herd confused." Milton felt that freedom should be in the hands of the intellectual aristocrat or the scholarly type.

Despite his contradictory feelings about freedom, Milton proceeded to write about the importance of a diversity of opinions and perspectives—the so-called "journalistic pluralism" so highly respected by American journalists today. For Milton, there must be open discussion (although presumably only among intellectuals); otherwise, many important ideas are lost forever, and truth cannot be unearthed. Contrary opinions are extremely valuable, according to Milton; without them society falls into a sickening conformity. Modern journalists would say "amen" to that sentiment. Many editorial and op-ed pages in newspapers and the variety of talk shows on radio and television today are memorials to this idea of Milton's.

As strong a spokesman for free expression as Milton was, his life testifies to the basic paradox of freedom. Inherent in us all and in all societies are the dualistic desires for freedom and an ordered society. Journalists know that freedom is valuable, but they also see the problems it can bring, the damage it can do, the injustices to which it can lead. When the Founding Fathers of the American Republic stated in 1791 that "Congress shall make no law . . . abridging the freedom of speech or of the press," they were undoubtedly wise, yet the thoughtful person knows that unlimited freedom of the press is not congenial to good social order.

Freedom is a valuable thing for the journalist to have, but it is not the only value and it must compete with others. It would be hard to believe that even Milton would favor unlimited freedom of the press, despite his ringing words in *Areopagitica.* Certainly Milton would have known that a righteous or good society involves more than the application of a single principle; it involves many principles in competition with one another. Milton's own life showed this clash of loyalties—to free expression and to the limitation of free expression for reasons he thought valid.

However, one must be careful in compromising freedom of expression. The well-known "foot in the door" problem can arise easily: Once you start tampering with freedom, restricting it for a greater good, then you may not know how to stop. Most journalists, even those who swear by the freedom statements of Milton, sense that the "social good" may often be something other than simply letting everyone say anything, anywhere, at any time.

In our heads, at least, we draw lines, fence freedom in, and propose exceptions to the tenet of free expression, as Milton did in his own life. The concept of the free marketplace of ideas is a noble one, but do we want to provide entry to all who want to display their wares? What about the wares of the advertiser who makes untrue claims for a product? What about a race-baiting group wanting to stir up community hostility and harm social stability? What about Justice Holmes' person who falsely shouts "fire!" in a crowded theater?

It is easy to see that we would make some kinds of restrictions on free expression—at least through the public media. And, of course, when we do make exceptions to free expression, we are indeed putting that foot in the door. The desire to exclude—to limit free expression in some way—is a natural step along the road of morality or ethics. It is an indication that a journalist, for instance, has gone beyond a simple love of freedom to a deep respect for the social good. It is, in fact, evidence of an ethical concern.

Milton, unfortunately, did not say much about ethics with respect to his protestations about the benefit of free expression and his condemnation of censorship. Today's journalist must assume that Milton, because of his religious zeal, would temper his freedom of expression with Christian moral principles. He would not, for instance, bear false witness (tell lies about someone), even if he were free to do so. The journalist looking to Milton for evidence that truth will win out in a fight with falsehood will not find it. Milton simply stated it, without proof.

Many philosophers, such as John Stuart Mill, have discarded Milton's idea as merely a rhetorical myth. Journalists, like all of us, would like to believe in this self-righting process. If we don't, we are committed to spending our lives never knowing the truth about anything, only hoping that one day it will manifest itself to us. If truth is as potent as Milton seemed to think it is, then surely we would know it when we see it. But do journalists recognize the truth? And do the consumers of journalism know it when they see it among all the information that is conveyed to them?

Milton didn't try to tackle such questions, and it's perhaps good that he didn't. For the idea of truth winning out over falsehood, myth though it may be, is a comforting one, and one that may serve as a catalyst for the journalist who, using freedom, at least tries to find the truth.

[9]

JOHN LOCKE

A pattern of responsible individualism, predicated on a love of reason and the importance of "natural law," was given an important impetus in 17th-century England by John Locke (1632–1704). He lived at a time when England was attempting great political reform, seeking to limit the power of the royalty, establish a parliament, and secure religious freedom. John Locke was a prime mover in these efforts—in both politics and philosophy.

His *Essay Concerning Human Understanding* (1690) is particularly significant in the development of empiricism, a philosophy that took over from the continental rationalism of Descartes. It deals with the concepts of certainty and the extent of human knowledge and also touches on belief, assent, and opinion, relating, of course, to epistemological concerns—such as truth and objectivity—dear to the journalist's heart. And in his *Two Treatises on Government,* published the same year, Locke argues that there is no divine right of kings and that people are free and equal in their natural state and have certain natural rights. These ideas had a great effect on both the American and French Constitutions.

Like all empiricists, Locke believed that human knowledge derives from sense experience, and he denied that ideas are innate in the human mind. He maintained that the human mind is a tabula rasa—a blank slate—written upon only by experience in the shape of reflections and sensations. Locke would likely tell modern journalists to throw themselves into reality, experiencing (and sensing) as many things and ideas as possible. Fill up the blank mind with data useful to the depiction of events: that would be his message to the reporter and analyst.

The Lockean journalist would not only be a person who gathers information; he or she would be concerned, intelligent, and rational and would see the wisdom in following rules. An existential note is struck by Locke in that he believed that each person is made of or constituted by actions and the awareness he or she has of the individualized self that those actions create. The moral journalist, Locke would say, is one who acts intentionally, after serious deliberation over what is right and good with respect to moral laws, which are ultimately founded in God's law.

A person cannot be ethical by chance, Locke is saying. And he would go further, seeming to contradict Aristotle and Confucius, and say that a person cannot act ethically simply out of habit. Moral (good) consequences can result from habitual action, but to act ethically a person must act self-consciously, recognizing fully that the actions stem from an understanding of right and wrong. The journalist, for instance, who habitually omits the name of a rape victim from a story without thinking about the situation and coming to a personal decision is simply acting automatically, not ethically.

Where does Locke get his moral injunctions or ethical guidelines? There are two sources, indicating two aspects of his character and value system: (1) One receives moral guidelines from the Bible, and (2) one discovers moral laws by using reason. These moral sources show Locke's dedication first to Christianity, and second to rationality. He would say that to be moral is to be rational. He would also say that moral rules are laws of nature, such laws being found in the Scriptures. But we can also get such rules from reason, and for Locke this would be the same as saying that we listen to the voice of God. However we might come by these ethical principles or rules, ultimately they come from God through the Scriptures or from God through our own reason. At any rate, Locke would say that to be moral is to be rational.

It is the responsibility of each person, says Locke, to follow the law of nature binding them to the preservation of peace and to a commitment not to harm one another. When people fail to do this, they institute governments and "contract" with one another to uphold the natural rights to life, liberty, and property. And Locke believed that if the ruler fails to protect these rights or misuses his power, the people are justified in removing him.

Locke was an early libertarian, believing that freedom is essential to the development of a full human being. Each person has a natural right to be free and not to be subjected to the will of another. Freedom, for Locke, is a "natural" right; freedom is good per se, not so that it might contribute to some social benefit, as John Stuart Mill would later assert. Of course, freedom for Locke is not complete because individuals live in a social context and need order, not anarchy, for their own well-being. Therefore, reason serves as an automatic limitation on freedom. In order to guide themselves in living an orderly and moral life, which is the essence of humanity, rational people voluntarily give up much freedom. This rational management of freedom, for Locke, is what differentiates humans from "the Savage Beasts" that live in a state "much beneath that of a Man."

Locke believed that freedom without reason was simply license. According to Locke, people are free by the law of nature, having inalienable rights to life, liberty, and property. But they also have the natural right to oppose and punish those who offend them or their possessions. Because some people, who are not reasonable, try to wield power over others and take away their natural rights, the necessity for battle or revolution may arise. Freedom without reason will lead to chaos and violent struggle. So freedom must be tempered by reason, and a person (read: journalist) would have no right to freedom unless it were guided by reason. Locke, then, was certainly not a "pure" libertarian. Very important strings were attached to his idea of freedom.

Perhaps the prime requisite for a person, in Locke's opinion, was reason. In fact, for him the test for participation in government was the possession of reason, not property, which he assumed everyone would have to varying degrees. Locke's view of human nature is optimistic, contrasting with the pessimistic view of his contemporary, Thomas Hobbes. Hobbes believed that society needed strong leadership and direction to keep the citizens under control; without a strong state human beings would act ferociously toward one another and would be constantly insecure. Locke, on the other hand, viewed citizens as being in a balanced and self-adjusting state, able to settle down and live harmoniously with little direction by government. Government would be needed mainly to provide safety for the citizens and stability for the state of nature.

Lockc pcrsonifies the liberal or libertarian point of view, whereas Hobbes is usually called conservative and even authoritarian. These two points of view—the libertarian and the authoritarian—are given classic expression in Locke's *Two Treatises* and Hobbes' *Leviathan*. Locke's ideas greatly influenced Jefferson and other American founders and formed an important part of American journalistic tradition, whereas Hobbes' perspective had a great effect on such thinkers as Rousseau, Stalin, Hitler, and other dictators.

Locke's concept of morality is derived from both reason and religion. Although God's explicit injunctions do not make up all of the moral truth, Locke does say that the foundation of such truth is found in the "Divine Law." Some moral truths, he says, are self-evident, found by the seeker through reason. Although Locke's idea of moral truth is rather hazy, it is based on Christian morality. He surely does not say that each person, for example, can define justice to suit his or her own purposes. Such a concept is not relative; it must stand on a solid foundation of Christian truth or on one, just as solid, of rationally inferred truth. And what is the source of this rational truth? Locke seems to say that it comes from education and from one's society. Part of the socialization process implies the acquisition of moral principles.

Locke, in various of his writings, gave some moral rules that he suggests comprise part of the natural law, knowable or discoverable through reason. Here are a few of them:

—Love and worship God
—Obey superiors
—Be friendly and mild and have a pure character
—Tell the truth and keep promises
—Do not injure, without cause, anyone's life or possessions
—Do not steal or kill
—Love your neighbor and your parents
—Help the distressed, and feed the hungry
—Preserve, nourish, and educate your children

These "natural rules" evidence Locke's reliance on the Bible for basic morality. But he would say that these are also *rational* rules that could be formulated even if there were no Bible. For him, they are "common sense" rules, practical rules, rules consistent with but not dependent on religious morality. Locke also speaks of three kinds of laws that guide actions: divine laws (enforced by God's eternal punishment or reward), civil laws (enforced by legal punishment), and laws of opinion (enforced by social pressure of praise or blame). All three of these types of laws contribute to the moral progress (fast, slow, or retrograde) of a person in society.

Now, what does the life and thought of Locke have to say to modern journalists? That they be moderate; that they not be absolutists; that they observe and communicate carefully; that they love freedom—for themselves and others; that they respect and study language and use it precisely; that they guard the concept that government should be by the consent of the governed but that corrupt leaders should be exorcised; that they have a happy, optimistic stance and an affinity for solutions as well as questions; that they be people of action, not simply rhetoric; that they be reasonable and thoughtful; that they have a religious grounding; and that they fight for the maximum individual liberty consistent with the welfare and rights of society.

John Locke, like John Milton a half century earlier, made strenuous efforts to terminate the British licensing system. He also prepared for the House of Commons a lengthy rationale for ending official censorship, and although he did not deal with press freedom specifically, he argued that the common law already protected society against irresponsible statements. His emphasis on the importance of property rights helped to link the concept of private ownership (of printing presses, for instance) to independence from government control. It was a big step for press freedom.

A respect for language, a love for empirical knowledge and its acquisition, a deep concern for ethical action, a desire for the rational and responsible use of freedom, and a basic concern for education—these traits and many others make John Locke one of history's greatest contributors to a legacy of wisdom for modern journalists.

[10]

VOLTAIRE

François-Marie Arouet Voltaire (1694–1778), of all the French *philosophes* of the 18th century, had the most to say to the modern journalist. He was a versatile writer—of novels, plays, political pamphlets, essays, and letters—who wished above all to provide an understanding of society and its needs and progress. Voltaire would have gained a solid place among journalists, if for no other reason, because of his famous maxim, "I disapprove of what you say but I will defend to the death your right to say it." This has become a kind of freedom-of-expression journalistic mantra, repeated over and over in press circles ever since.

Voltaire was a wide-ranging writer of some 100 volumes, with eclectic interests and an acerbic style, and one who distrusted unsubstantiated information. One lesson he can provide to journalists and all writers by his own example is, Work hard! He believed that not to be occupied is not to exist. He opined that the only people who are not good are the idle. Voltaire surely personified the diligence, rationalism, and concern with a polemical style of his age. Victor Hugo remarked that Voltaire characterized the entire 18th century.

This fiery Frenchman was a fighter. With his earthy humor and skepticism, he fought superstition and corruption; he fought the excesses of government and Church; and he provided the intellectual powder for such revolutionaries as Robespierre and Danton to bring down the French regime during the French Revolution. He had great influence during his 83 years of life. Despite exile, imprisonment, and the suppression of many of his books, he persistently satirized social injustice and pushed reason and education as the driving force behind political change.

In his 1737 *Lettre à un journaliste,* he urged journalists to write clearly, directly, and with a style that gained and kept the attention of readers while at the same time inspiring trust. Voltaire certainly practiced this in his own writing; it is commonly agreed that he writes so well that one fails to realize he is writing philosophy. Good writing, he believed, is good writing, and he would certainly advise the journalist to write better than anyone else.

Voltaire also thought that journalists should be skeptical, never believing anything without checking it out for themselves. And he consistently extolled the value of freedom of expression. Especially in his popular *Philosophical Dictionary* (a collection of articles by liberal writers throughout the ages), Voltaire ruminated on the value of press freedom in an essay of his own in which he articulately opposed the idea of censorship and touted the free voice of reason.

A social reformer, Voltaire saw his task (like that of the other *philosophes,* such as Montesquieu, Rousseau, Helvétius, and Bayle) as demolishing the old system and constructing a new one. To do this, he developed a superlatively honed method of satire, challenging accepted ideas by making them seem ridiculous. Such satire was urbane, even cosmopolitan, and assumed opponents who were civilized and sensitive enough to discern the barrage of wit being used. Voltaire felt that holding something up to ridicule assumes a respect for reason among all parties concerned, and he considered reasonableness a prerequisite for satire.

The arena most popular for Voltaire's satire was religion (he disliked organized religion and championed religious tolerance), but he used it in other areas also. Poke fun at ideas and people, said Voltaire, and do it in a way to make a serious point. Show up the absurdities in society. Ridicule villains in a light style with unexpected barbs hidden in it. Deal with subjects imaginatively, in unexpected ways, subjecting them to a careful empiricism and critical analysis. Use scientific methods, when possible. And, said Voltaire, make careful observations and be precise in your transcribing of direct quotations and other pertinent data. Voltaire was greatly influenced by Locke, Hume, and other British empiricists, and his scientific stance had a profound influence on later journalism.

But despite his scientific inclinations, Voltaire firmly believed in colorful writing, refusing to get bogged down in simply a collection of dry facts. He was mainly writing history, but he could have been writing journalism. He thought one's writing should be amusing and lively. Although substance, to Voltaire, was exceedingly important, he was, of all the French writers of his day, particularly infatuated with style. For him, the writer had two main duties: Never to slander, and never to bore. Voltaire was never boring, and his empiricism, usually tinged with satire and wit, was never pedantic or mean-spirited. Today's journalists can learn much by reading his books and essays.

A kind of counterpoint to Voltaire and his rationalism was Jean Jacques Rousseau, who was injecting a new romanticism into France. Educator Will Durant (in his *Story of Philosophy*) wrote that the "complex soul of France seemed to have divided itself into these two men, so different and yet so French." Here was Voltaire exemplifying the intellect, and here was Rousseau extolling instinct. Whereas Voltaire always championed reason, Rousseau had little faith in it. Voltaire believed society must be managed; Rousseau thought that laws should be removed so that citizens could reach a state of equality.

When Rousseau sent Voltaire his *Discourse on the Origin of Inequality,* Voltaire thanked him in a 1765 letter for his "new book against the human species . . . with its arguments against civilization, letters, and science, and for a return to the natural condition as seen in savages and animals." And Voltaire was saddened to see Rousseau's love for the natural state of nature resumed in *The Social Contract.* He wrote to a friend that Rousseau resembled a philosopher as a monkey resembled a man. But at the same time he attacked the Swiss authorities for burning the book.

Voltaire had aristocratic tastes, and the idea of democracy in the modern sense was alien to him. Many of his letters refer to the "rabble," the masses that he and his fellow *philosophes* felt should not have the vote. In fact, in a letter to Frederick the Great, Voltaire wrote of the rabble as not worthy of enlightenment. Voltaire was a strange kind of "democratic" revolutionary; he knew reform was needed in French society, but he favored its being instituted from above.

The American founders, especially Jefferson, admired Voltaire greatly. Obviously they selectively found in Voltaire's writing that which they could endorse. Voltaire's disdain for the "stupid and barbarous" masses, for example, surely would not have inspired Jefferson and his fellow revolutionaries. But Voltaire's support for freedom of expression and his deep love of reason had a great appeal for these early American thinkers and political reformers. Jefferson and his friends had the deepest respect for John Locke, and, as Voltaire's ideas were similar to Locke's, it is natural that the Americans would have an affinity for the Frenchman.

Voltaire, often considered a pessimist, thought of himself as a realist. Although it is true that he did not have an optimistic outlook, he did not succumb to despair. He was an activist and believed that people make themselves through action, through involvement in the events of society. In this sense, he showed some important existentialist tendencies that were to manifest themselves later in French philosophical circles. Although he liked action, Voltaire also loved the thoughtful, peaceful, bookish life.

A fellow *philosophe* of Voltaire's, Claude-Adrien Helvétius, had brought from England the utilitarian ideas of David Hume that helped free morality from the bonds of religion and place it in the purview of secular rational thought. Virtue, according to Hume and Helvétius, consisted largely in seeking pleasure and avoiding pain; happiness needed to be maximized in society—that was the essence of virtue or morality. Helvétius introduced such ideas to France and dealt with them in his *On the Mind*

(1758), antagonizing the worlds of religion and philosophy. The book was condemned by the authorities at the Sorbonne and burned a year later by an edict of Parliament. In 1765, seven years after its publication, it was again condemned, this time by the Church's national assembly. Voltaire himself was angered by the book's secular emphasis and materialism, and he let Helvétius know in no uncertain terms that he disagreed with him, but at the same time he penned his famous line about being willing to defend until death Helvétius' right to say what he did.

Voltaire was interested in practical matters, and he did much to instill in French thought the importance of changing the social system and reforming the old regime. The middle class was especially eager to respond in some way to the absolutism of Louis XIV, which had placed France in a political and moral weak state. It was Voltaire (and other 18th-century *philosophes*) who provided the intellectual support for the economic and political change being advocated by many practical people of the middle class. The spirit of empiricism and the great faith in reason, which Voltaire had brought from England and planted in French intellectual soil, proved strong indeed and focused the light of publicity on unjust laws, social evils, and religion.

This rationalism and empiricism, like the journalism that Voltaire advocated throughout his life, stirred the people and created a mood of reasoned dissent from traditional authority. Voltaire never advocated revolution; his idea was for rational, evolutionary reform of the system. But Voltaire and the other *philosophes* planted the seeds of revolution, and the impatient French, finding more reasonable reform unsuccessful, turned to more violent and extreme means: the French Revolution.

[11]

DAVID HUME

A society's customs, not reason, will tell us what is socially ethical; a person's perceptions and impressions will tell him or her what is individually ethical—this is the basis of the ethics of the Scottish philosopher David Hume (1711–1776). Probably the leading British thinker of the 18th century, Hume was the consummate skeptic and relativist, rejecting absolutes and believing that ethics arose from social conventions and not from following a priori principles.

According to Hume we cannot know anything with certainty, and this relates also to what is right and wrong. We are always searching, garnering only bits and pieces of "the truth," which we intermingle with our impressions and perceptions to give us our own truth, and moral guidance, by which we must live. For Hume, impressions are powerful, even more powerful than ideas. In the field of ethics this would translate into acting on impressions, hunches, whims, or the particular situation and circumstances.

His main work, *A Treatise of Human Nature* (1740), in which he presented his main philosophy of skepticism, was not popular, and Hume was generally criticized for more than a century in England. In America, however, his influence was felt among early thinkers. In Germany, Immanuel Kant felt the effect of Hume's thought, but it led him to react against Hume and develop a system of ethical deontology that turned Hume's skeptical and relativistic thought upside down.

Without realizing it, Hume, an Enlightenment philosopher, was abandoning the Aristotelian heritage of rationalism, of science, of knowing, of objectivism (although he remained close to Aristotle in ethics) and was serving to usher in the sense-related romanticism that was to spring up in England and on the Continent.

Hume had no faith in either the senses or reason to provide reliable knowledge. Such extreme skepticism leaves a person in a kind of unintelligible universe, knowing nothing for certain and hoping that useful insights can be found in the swirl of perceptions and impressions. Hume's philosophy comes from the basic empiricist principle that nothing is in the mind that is not first sensed by the senses.

Enthroning perceptions, Hume was always the empiricist who doubted that we could know that even a "self" or personal identity exists outside our various perceptions. And he would say that there is no need to try to anticipate the future; it is not "perceivable." We come to conclusions only from what we perceive, or what we "feel" or "intuit" or "opine." We never really know anything; we simply give preference to one set of arguments or impressions over another.

Journalists are probably Humeans to some degree because they are inclined in the direction of skepticism. They are certainly empiricists, perceiving various events around them and reporting (and discussing) these impressions at great length. What they hope, of course, is that from this variety and maze of impressions and journalistic perceptions the truth will emerge—at least to a considerable degree and with some validity.

As for ethics, Hume would say that there exist no rational principles of good and bad. As a skeptic, he saw something that is good for one person as not necessarily being good for another. No Kantian a priori maxims for Hume, no universal moral laws, no reliable guidelines for our ethical conduct. Morality is simply a matter of personal preference, a matter of our feelings and not our intellect. As Hume wrote in Part III of *A Treatise of Human Nature,* "Moral good and evil are certainly distinguished by our *sentiments,* not by *reason.*" When these sentiments of many people coalesce, then custom arises, and only custom can direct us in the way we should go. Such an ethical theory appeals to many journalists today who wish to satisfy convention: What most people feel to be right is right, and what most people feel to be wrong is wrong. These journalists should remember, however, that Hume put great stock in *character,* in being a person of virtue who is courageous, self-respecting, kind, and just.

Hume believed in what might be called a democratic ethics, the type of theory that holds that actions are good or right if a majority of people feel they are good and right—a kind of majoritarian approval rationale for ethics. Hume said that actions which brought about pleasant consequences were the ones which received this social approval. One can see here the stirrings of utilitarianism. Considering majority opinion as the "right" opinion—or even consequences to the majority as the "best" consequences—is, of course, open to objection. A minority is sometimes right; a majority can be wrong.

Many may wonder how Hume balanced his majoritarian test for ethics with his emphasis on individual virtues and character development. And this is, indeed, rather puzzling. Perhaps Hume thought that the majority will somehow reflect the "good" that is evidenced in the lives of virtuous individuals. It would be a mistake to think of Hume as having no concern for what people actually *do* as they aspire to be moral. But doing springs from being, and Hume was, indeed, more concerned with what people *are*—in their basic character. In fact, like Aristotle, he considered character as the moral end and stressed self-respect, urging people to survey their own lives and conduct to see whether they are worthy of respect. And again like Aristotle, he put emphasis on the virtues—not on the specific acts, but on the total self-respecting *self* out of which these acts arise. A deserved pride and self-esteem, for Hume, is the crown jewel of character and the highest of all the virtues.

At any rate, we can see that Hume, despite his general relativist outlook, did believe in some "general and inflexible principles" that would keep society from falling into anarchy and disorder. One of these is undoubtedly the principle of majoritarian happiness brought on by "democratic ethics" mentioned above. Hume did not specify or explicate these general rules, but it is clear that he did believe in some rules "wherever men have any intercourse with each other." So it must be said that he was not the complete relativist he is often pictured as being, and certainly the bridge between his general relativism and Kant's ethical formalism is more sturdy than usually envisioned.

Hume viewed people as being motivated by their own self-interests. Like Thomas Hobbes before him and Ayn Rand two centuries later, Hume saw the basic pull of egoism and the natural desire to pursue one's own self-interests, to avoid pain and to seek happiness. In fact, his emphasis on the human proclivity to be happy was instrumental in the development of utilitarianism and the teleological ethical theory of Jeremy Bentham and John Stuart Mill.

In today's dialogues about ethics, the descendants of Hume would probably be called "non-cognitive ethicists," meaning that statements that assert what is right to do or what is not right to do are neither true nor false. Such statements do not belong to the realm of knowledge: They are beyond truth or falsity; they are simply expressions of personal taste or sentiment. Thus, they are non-cognitive. They indicate personal opinion or prejudice and are relative to the whims, impulses, or desires of the individual. There is no need to try to find *truth* in them. They are simply personal value judgments.

In political philosophy as it impinges on ethics, Hume used the family as analogous to what a good state should be. The family is both selfish and imbued with sympathetic understanding, and parents control their children through using both the stick and carrot, through showing harshness and sympathy, firmness and concern. There is no reason to think that Hume would not apply this to the running of a modern newspaper or television station. However, even if he did, he would certainly say that such a formula might not be appropriate for every medium.

Hume was sympathetic to what we call an "open society" and defended civil liberties, seeing press freedom as no real threat to rulers. Even if press freedom is abused, the reading of books, pamphlets, or newspapers cannot inflame the public, he would say, and cannot endanger society. Hume would see the reader as reading alone, detached and receiving impressions "coolly," so incitement to action is highly unlikely. Hume, of course, was aware only of print media, and it is probable that he would consider television and radio as far more inflammatory and potentially disruptive of a society's stability.

The journalist of today who is basically skeptical and relativistic would find Hume a valuable teacher. But even Hume's relativism is relativistic in that there seem to be some standards and limits he would accept, although he does not delineate just what they would be. The journalist who is concerned with consequences—especially with making decisions that will maximize happiness—will find an affinity with Hume as well as with John Stuart Mill. And the journalist who is suspicious of "all truths," all authorities, all certainties will find Hume congenial. But Hume was a complex thinker, as are all great thinkers, and would say that any perception of him is no more than a quick insight that will lead to an impression, not a true image. This skeptical concept, in itself, can be most valuable to the journalist who, as an empiricist, tries to turn impressions into stories.

[12]

IMMANUEL KANT

Immanuel Kant (1724–1804), one of the premier German philosophers, is usually considered history's best example of a deontological (legalistic, law-oriented) ethicist. He believed that only an action taken out of self-imposed duty could be ethical and that any consideration of consequences either to self or to others would nullify the action's moral substance.

Kant would tell journalists to have some a priori principles, rules, or maxims to which they feel duty-bound to follow. These would be absolute rational principles that serve as guides to ethical behavior. Kantian journalists would not act so as to bring about some kind of consequence; rather, they would simply act in accordance with duty to a guiding principle. For Kant, morality is to be completely separated from any desire to achieve pleasure or happiness either for self or for others. An ethical maxim or rule is categorical, binding us unconditionally in an a priori manner.

Seeing this principle-oriented ethics as a kind of radical freedom, Kant would say that when a journalist, for example, is dedicated to duty to a maxim or ethical rule, that person is freed from all natural motives and considerations that will in a sense imprison him or her in a ceaseless lockstep of moral relativity and consequence prediction. Having a priori journalistic principles, freely and rationally accepted, will liberate the journalist and lead to ethical actions. If journalists follow their rationally accepted principles, then they are ethical; if not, they are unethical. It's as simple as that. Kant would tell the journalist that it is ethically unproductive to make exceptions, to be inconsistent in following these duties or "categorical imperatives," as he called them. There are other kinds of imperatives, Kant believed, called "hypothetical imperatives," but these are things one must do to achieve some particular end. And according to Kant, they are pragmatic in nature, not ethical.

A categorical duty would be one that, regardless of the agent's particular desire, should be done. Such a duty binds a journalist, for example, simply because it is rational and freely accepted. Such ethical "oughts" stem from Kant's categorical imperative, a principle that he believed all rational people would accept. This super-maxim or imperative (see Kant's *Foundations of the Metaphysics of Morals*) went like this: "Act only according to that maxim by which you can at the same time will that it should become universal law."

Kant also enthroned people as people, and his second formulation of the categorical imperative demanded that each person should be treated as a person and not as a means to some end. A basic respect for people, a sincere valuation of human dignity, and a consistency in following rational maxims: these were the foundation stones of Kant's ethical system. Certainly the Machiavellian journalist would not feel an affinity for Kantian ethics.

Kant believed that moral perfection is perfection that is not merely disinterested but *uninterested* loyalty to the law. This would mean a kind of selflessness untarnished by a concern for self-pleasure or for consequences to others. To some degree Kant was an ethical innovator: His formalistic ethics was perhaps the first to recommend an uncompromising philosophy of self-sacrifice. His view was that other ethicists actually were talking about pragmatics and dealing in rationalizations, not ethics. They really had not discovered morality. Why? Because they never saw ethics as a matter of duty, seeing it only as a need for action from some vested interest and hoping for a certain result.

Journalists usually find Kant's philosophy a little too cold, formalistic, and binding for them. Many, however, do try to be Kantians, having strongly held beliefs about their journalistic responsibilities. Telling the truth, for instance, or always giving the source of quotes. But the Kantian road is a difficult one, and most journalists wander away from it often. And as they do, they make exceptions, have double standards, and often seem inconsistent in their ethical activity.

Kant denied all teleological theories of ethics (those holding that an action is ethical because it leads to certain consequences). He said, instead, that nothing is good except a good will, for all other types of goodness are dependent on conditions and situations. A main criticism of this Kantian view is that his moral law is, indeed, itself subject to a condition: that of being apprehended by a rational mind. Both a "good will" and a rationally determined action that could be universal would, of course, be contingent on the degree of rationality of the particular person. One might doubt that all "rational" journalists, for example, would come to the same maxim vis-à-vis the printing of the names of rape victims or sources of information.

Despite considerable semantic difficulty with Kant's ideas, the basic concept of guiding principles in ethics is firmly rooted in American journalism. Most journalists do have guiding principles, and they want to be known as "principled" journalists. But they seem to have little trouble in departing from these principles, in rationalizing them away, and in considering consequences either to themselves or to others in their actions.

If Kant were the editor of an American newspaper, he would undoubtedly expect all rational staffers (and he would probably screen them himself before hiring them) to follow certain journalistic principles in every situation, not just when it suited them. If, for example, a fundamental maxim of a reporter or of the newspaper were to fully disclose information that had been verified, then the reporter would be bound by duty-to-principle to do so in every case, not just in some cases.

What Kant would say to his staffers would be something like this: Test your principle against the categorical imperative (would you want such a principle to be universal?) and stick to it come whatever, not worrying about the possible consequences but letting the chips fall where they may. What you are, Kant would say, is a truth-teller, a full-disclosure reporter, and you shouldn't worry about the results of your journalistic action. When you start thinking about possible consequences, you will start fudging the truth, tampering with verified facts, and therefore you will be a dishonest reporter.

(Note that the terms "truth-teller" and "full-disclosure reporter" probably would not be used by Kant. In all likelihood he would not say that the journalist should, or could, present the "truth" in any kind of objective sense. For, in epistemology, Kant was an idealist, believing that people, things, or events could not be reported "in themselves." They are unknowable, and what the journalist could do would be only to provide a world of appearances that are not actually real. Kant would say that the journalist's mind filters or structures material it gets from reality and presents this shadowy world of appearances to the audience.)

As noted above, Kant's ethics is difficult, and many depart from it. But his ethical foundation for journalism is also firm and principled and has a great appeal for many people. It gives specific guidance to journalists before an ethical quandary appears. And it is a foundational moral theory that gives a clear-cut answer to the question: Have I been ethical? If one of my journalistic maxims is that I will not tamper with direct quotes, for example, and I do change words or otherwise alter the quotes, then I have forsaken my maxim and am guilty of unethical behavior.

Most journalists, however, tend to think that if they are to act ethically, they will need to consider the effects or results of their actions. They feel that simply acting out of duty or respect for a law is shallow and makes the journalist no more than a moral robot devoid of any reasons for ethical action. This idea of compliance with the law in itself, which Kant suggested, does not set well with many free-wheeling, individualistic journalists desiring ad hoc solutions to moral quandaries.

Kant was rather specific about his concept of dedication to duty, to the need to follow a priori moral laws. Here are Kant's own words from *Foundations (or Fundamental Principles) of the Meta-*

physics of Morals (T. K. Abbott, translator; London: Longmans Green, 1927, pp. 16–17):

> The moral worth of an action does not lie in the effect expected from it, nor in any principle of action which requires to borrow its motive from this expected effect. . . . The preeminent good which we call moral can . . . consist in nothing else than *the conception of law* in itself, which certainly is only possible in a rational being, in so far as this conception, and not the expected effect, determines the will. This is a good which is already present in the person who acts accordingly, and we have not to wait for it to appear first in the result.

The journalist who would follow Kantian ethics should recognize the importance of duty. More than almost any other thinker, Kant is identified with this emphasis. He did not talk about divine commands, for he was interested in ethics, not theology. As a man of the Enlightenment, he made reason, not God, the source of moral law. Reason, however, would come before the formulation of categorical maxims; then these maxims would guide ethical behavior.

A journalist of the teleological persuasion, a Utilitarian for instance, might well insist that his or her ethics was rational also; but it is a kind of ad hoc rationality tied to a consideration or projection of consequences in specific cases. Kant would have solved this problem ahead of time; he would have rationally determined which principles or maxims would guide him so that when ethical decisions posed themselves, he would have a ready answer for them.

What we probably find most frequently in journalism are journalists who are part Kantian and part consequentialist. They may be fundamentally Kantian in that they accept basic rules, maxims, and principles in their journalism to which they feel duty-bound in general. But they feel that they must, on occasion, make exceptions, consider alternatives and special circumstances. In short, they must be free, after serious thinking, to deviate from their generally accepted principle and to take what they think at the time is a higher ethical action. So they may see themselves as fundamentally Kantian but of the type who do not cease to "think" after they have a guiding foundational principle.

This synthesis of deontology and teleology, which has been called "deontelic ethics" (Merrill, *The Dialectic in Journalism,* LSU Press, 1989), is probably a widely accepted stance. However, it may well be no more than a rationalization and departs from the essential ethical legalistic system of Kant. It is likely that most philosophers would say that the journalist who tries to combine Kantianism with utilitarianism, for example, is simply an inauthentic journalist who will make up rules as he or she goes along. It might be only a way of trying to please two ethical gods—duty and self-determination. And for Kant, this simply will not work.

During the late 19th century and well into the 20th, Kant's idea of an innate, absolute moral sense lost adherents. Increasingly, ethicists have discarded Kant's philosophy for a more evolutionary one that sees morality as conduct more or less determined by a need for social survival. Contrary to Kant's belief, the idea has arisen that no action is good in itself. Ethics, then, is now largely tied to motivations and consequences.

But out of this reaction against Kantian legalism various rumblings are being heard, still soft but getting louder, which suggest that perhaps a need exists for some kind of more absolute and "duty-oriented" ethics. As modern journalists, among others, are swamped in the waves of relativism and uncertainty about ethics and as untempered individualism threatens to undermine social stability, perhaps the day is not far off when a disintegrating world will again welcome Immanuel Kant's call to duty.

[13]

EDMUND BURKE

A thoughtful, courageous, and social utilitarian orientation was provided by the Irish statesman and philosopher Edmund Burke (1729–1797), who would see modern journalism's main responsibility as preserving peace and harmony and protecting the society that grants it freedom. Here was a great thinker who synthesized the antinomies of freedom and responsibility in his basic philosophy and action. Burke had much to say about freedom, responsibility, and truth—concepts vital to the journalist's role.

Burke, in many ways, would be a modern conservative; in other ways, he would be a modern liberal. He had strains of the authoritarian in him, but he also exemplified characteristics of the libertarian. Probably in today's world he would be closer to the advocate of social responsibility in journalism. For Burke, promoting social stability and national security by respecting tradition and social morality would largely define responsibility for the mass media.

Although he would not want government-controlled media, Burke would argue that the press has a basic responsibility to help maintain social order and that such maintenance is more important than trying to be "fair" or "objective." Burke saw eternal law based on Judeo-Christian values and historical tradition as the foundation of social stability and progress. Like Confucius and Aristotle, he valued social "habits"—customs, prejudices, and institutions. He was opposed to the French Revolution, and one reason was that it sought to uproot basic religious and moral traditions and convictions. Burke felt that such revolutionary change is never good; social change should be slow and carefully planned.

Edmund Burke was born in Dublin in 1729 to a Catholic mother and Protestant father and grew up in a working-class family. He was graduated from Trinity College, Dublin, in 1748. In 1765 Burke was elected to Parliament and served for nearly 30 years as a controversial but highly respected member. One of Parliament's most gifted orators and catalytic writers, he established himself as one of the leading thinkers of 18th-century Britain.

Burke was greatly disturbed by the upheaval in France brought on by the revolutionists, and his *Reflections on the Revolution in France* (1790) is perhaps one of the most eloquent and passionate criticisms of this traumatic episode in European history. He saw the revolution as not simply an overthrow of the Bourbon monarchy but more importantly as a rejection of European morality and civilized tradition. Until his dying day, Burke criticized the French Revolution, seeing it as a warning to future generations who, in the hope of getting more freedom, would promote the idea that a society would be better off without the strictures of social customs and habits.

Although he would certainly support the idea of social responsibility in modern journalism, Burke manifested many traits of the libertarian. He was extremely suspicious of power, being familiar with the harm it can cause if misused. He would urge the journalist to expose such misuse of power, foster social stability, emphasize tradition and civility, and oppose abrupt and traumatic change. As for quick fixes and sudden change in journalism itself, Burke would urge caution; he would propose that novel new concepts of journalism, although made by brilliant thinkers, cannot compare in validity with practices that are a result of viability through many generations. If institutions are to change, they should change slowly and deliberately. Change for the sake of change, he would say, is senseless and dangerous.

Burke would see journalists as defenders of social morality, with the power to bless or curse people and ideas that burst on the scene. Therefore, journalists become the arbiters of good and evil, subtly but consistently determining a country's value system. Playing up the actions of controversial figures (such as Madonna, Dr. Jack Kevorkian, or David Koresh) would be counterproductive and socially irresponsible journalism to Burke. He would, like the Hutchins Commission that studied the press in the 1940s, want to see more serious, socially relevant, and positive news and interpretation emphasized. Burke would probably frown on the titillating tabloid journalism of today, seeing it devoid of any contribution to civilized discourse, thoughtful analysis, or moral significance.

Journalism, from a Burkean perspective, would be expected to preserve and strengthen what Burke called the four "essential links" of father, family, place, and property that connect people and form a viable and healthy society. He saw these essential links as permanent and derived from a divine origin. Today, they may seem outmoded, but Burke gave them great significance. He would say that journalism should do everything possible to uphold these values because they are the essence of society and the foundation for personal stability and morality. Fathers develop a sense of respect for oneself; families provide a sense of identity; place (work) also contributes to identity and self-worth; and the right to own property links one to the past, present, and future.

Burke was always concerned with good manners. He believed that manners can and should be harmonized with morality. Probably nobody in modern times has been more convinced of the importance of good manners than Edmund Burke. He believed that manners are even more important than laws, for he saw laws as largely dependent on manners. Here is some of what he wrote about manners in *Letters on a Regicide Peace* (1796): "Manners are what vex or soothe, corrupt or purify, exalt or debase, barbarize or refine us, by a constant, steady, uniform, insensible operation, like that of the air we breathe in. They give their whole form and color to our lives. According to their quality, they aid morals, they supply them, or they totally destroy them."

Journalists could take these words seriously and use them

in their own ethics. Such habitual manners as showing patience, consistency, thoughtfulness, empathy, care, respect, and promptness will mix well into a journalist's overall moral philosophy and ease ethical decision making. In fact, as Confucius and Aristotle had stressed much earlier, manners undergird morality and make it largely instinctual.

Reflecting some of the thoughts of Milton before him and Mill after, Burke considered a pluralism (even a competition) of opinions and ideas of great value. He would suggest a competitive, dialectic attitude for journalists. Competition, Burke thought, was an incentive to innovation and improvement and a spur to quality. Critics of competition argue that it brings about enmity; but Burke said that on the contrary, competition brings about rivalry, emulation, and stimulation. Such competition would be good among units in a press system and also within a single mass medium in which internal competition among staff members would lead to improved quality.

Competitive efforts in journalism, Burke would say, would be beneficial to the individuals involved, to the quality of the medium and to the press, and ultimately to the whole society. Competition is a stimulus to quality and should be encouraged. Writing of competition, Burke noted that when we meet competition our nerves are strengthened and our skills sharpened. Always, he said, we should consider our antagonist as our helper.

If Burke were a modern news reporter concerned with the *who, what, when, why,* and *how* of journalism, he would probably emphasize *why,* giving increased attention to the background of the story. Then, that done, he would focus on the ramifications to society, looking carefully at the potential social harm or social good that might accrue from publishing the story. This kind of reporting is interesting, for it would give serious attention both to history and to the future. Certainly its future emphasis could be called social-consequence reporting (social teleology); but it would also be a form of historical analysis intended to shed light on the *why* of the present event and on the possible future consequences. The rather simplistic facts of the present event would, for Burke, take an incidental or subordinate position to the historical and futuristic implications.

This kind of journalistic emphasis would have a relation to the "truth" of the story. Burke would have journalists discover the truth (or a large part of it) for themselves—looking carefully, not only at the event, but casting an analytical eye backward into the past and forward into the future. Truth, for Burke as for all other serious thinkers, is complex and multifaceted, but he would see it largely as a representation of those aspects of the reality of the story that would bring the best results for society. This socially pragmatic concept of truth for the news reporter would probably not be generally acceptable, but Burke would see it as the kind of responsible journalism required of a rational press.

Ethical concepts would, for Burke, place considerable limits on press freedom. A concern for ethics naturally leads to restraining certain journalistic actions, omitting certain facts, giving subjective emphasis and de-emphasis to various aspects of the story, quoting and not quoting certain sources. In other words, ethics demands a voluntary decision to curb one's natural inclinations or freedom. Burke would see ethics as a voluntary controlling mechanism, and moral decision making presupposes the imposition of various kinds of restrictions on one's journalism. Burke would see journalistic self-management not only as a legitimate practice but a socially responsible one that should occur any time a journalist selects a story and determines its design. The requirement: to protect social stability and security and raise the moral and intellectual level of the audience.

For many of today's journalists, this philosophy would seem heretical. It would be too similar to what many see as the incipient authoritarianism of the 1947 Hutchins Commission. They would like the idea of editorial self-determination but would balk at such determination being predicated on social stability and security. This, they would probably feel, strays too far from traditional press libertarianism. But Burke was touting a responsible use of freedom, and one that had society's needs in mind.

In conclusion, it can be said that Edmund Burke was thinking of a meaningful truth as superior to accurate facts, and he was thinking of a socially responsible use of freedom as superior to the simple libertarian concept of freedom as nothing more than a natural right. These and other seminal ideas of the influential Irish thinker are ones the modern journalist might do well to consider carefully.

[14]

ARTHUR SCHOPENHAUER

Despite the fact that the German philosopher Arthur Schopenhauer (1788–1860) is the most pessimistic and perhaps the most mystical of eminent European thinkers, he did have some insights into journalism that might be helpful, or at least thought-provoking. Certainly his acerbic criticism of newspapers (which he also could have made of broadcasting) might cause journalists to take a closer look at themselves. He referred to newspapers as the second hand on history's clock, saying that this hand was of inferior metal to the other two and did not often work properly.

Other opinions about journalism that he presented in his *Essays and Aphorisms* are that exaggeration is essential to newspaper writing, and journalists are alarmists, resembling little dogs who start barking as soon as something moves. He had other things to say about journalism, but they don't get any better. In general, he said, the newspaper is like a magnifying glass—or more correctly, perhaps, like a shadow flickering on a wall.

Schopenhauer saw journalism as history written quickly, and he had hardly more respect for history. Although he saw some value in history, as he did journalism, he felt it was an inferior rival to philosophy. In the same way as he saw journalism, he found history to be little more than a repetition of the same events, "as when a kaleidoscope is turned you see only the same things in differing configurations." Here he deals with something heard many times today in criticisms of journalism: that the news concentrates on fleeting particulars and presents bits and pieces of unsynthesized reality.

Schopenhauer's philosophy is complex and impossible to capture in a short sketch, but it was a mixture of Kantian idealism and Hindu mysticism. He was probably the West's most pronounced intuitionist, not only in metaphysics but also in morality. He had little faith in rationalism, believed Aristotelian logic (the "either/or") to be defective, and thought that a proper substitute for fathoming reality was intuition. Schopenhauer considered this intuitionism to be true, although it was unfortunately incommunicable. At least we can say that he exalted feeling and mistrusted reason. His basic perspective was poetic or religious rather than prosaic and scientific.

For Schopenhauer it was important for a person to develop the inner, unmediated, continuous, and dynamic part of the self. The thing that stands between a person and an intuitive understanding of reality is what he called the will. He explicates this difficult concept in *The World as Will and Idea* (1818). The lower form of mind is will; the higher form he called intellect. And, perhaps for him, an even higher form might be called instinct or a kind of transcendental aesthetic appreciation. The natural world was what he called will, and the world of ideas was created by the intellect. The world of aesthetic, meditative happiness was brought about by subduing the will. The restless and always-seeking will must be suppressed, Schopenhauer said, and a person needs to be devoted to intellectual and aesthetic contemplation. We must, like the Buddhist seeking Nirvana, suppress desire and thereby transcend such concepts as good and bad, better and worse, right and wrong.

Schopenhauer would urge today's journalists to immerse themselves in the great books—works that impart wisdom. But they should value the contents, not the books themselves. Ideas, concepts, and the inner life are more important than material goods. He would recommend seeking happiness within ourselves rather than relying on things others might give us. Our world is shaped, he said, by the way we look at it; therefore, it is essential for people to develop a consciousness and self-sufficiency that will sustain them. A person who constantly contemplates life as rising above desiring objects is one who breaks the pattern of endless willing and achieves happiness and freedom. The will must be tamed or extinguished, and the journalist who can be freed from it can see the world clearly, recognizing that what had been significant is really insignificant.

The journalist who desires to be accepted by society and who diligently climbs the ladder of success is one who, for Schopenhauer, is basically a failure. He believed that a person is generally sociable to the extent to which he or she is intellectually and aesthetically poor. Excellent or quality people, he said, do not need the company of others nor the material products of the world nearly so much as do people who are unsure and dissatisfied with themselves. Reflecting his interest in Oriental philosophy, Schopenhauer believed that the person who learns to contemplate the beauty and consolation received from nature and art can overlook the cares of life, be happy, and see the world more clearly.

Intuition is important to Schopenhauer. An internal or intuitive perspective on the world is more real than one that is rational and external. He said that the intellect divides everything, but that intuition unites everything. The journalist of a Schopenhauerian bent will trust intuition and try to develop aesthetic proclivities. Intellectualism will not do; instinct is more basic than reason. The ultimate good is beauty, and the ultimate happiness lies in creating, cherishing, and enjoying the beautiful.

In a real sense Schopenhauer's ethics and his aesthetics commingle. His ethical stance is dependent on the degree to which one can extinguish one's will, cease personal striving and competition, and merge oneself into the aesthetic world. An egoistic or altruistic ethics? Schopenhauer would not put such a question. His ethics would be a kind of transcendent ethics that would dissolve into a kind of non-ethics, for he would eliminate the ego and also would not worry about altruistic activity. An appreciation of aesthetics—a love of art—can push us temporarily into a realm where will is sublimated, where our restless pursuits are stilled and our desires are washed away. But this is only a first stage in Schopenhauer's becoming one with the world.

So far as Schopenhauer has a moral theory, it might be said

to include a breaking away from a kind of Hobbesian egoism, in which everyone wars against everyone else. The next stage is one in which a person realizes that there are other wills in the world and that others, too, are desiring creatures. The person's pure egoism is replaced in this stage by a sense of justice and equality and a concern for his or her fellows. And finally, there are some people who are able to move into the saintliness of the Christian or Hindu realm where a kind of contemplative peacefulness dominates and a cessation of striving, desiring, and competing leaves the person in the calm eddies of transcendent morality. Thus, for Schopenhauer, the absence of all egoistic motivation is the main indication of moral worth.

In short, at Schopenhauer's final stage the will has been eliminated, and the individual becomes part of all and all becomes part of the individual. At this final and highest stage of moral development a person attains voluntary renunciation, resignation, and complete will-lessness. To some degree we see here a final stage similar to Kierkegaard's final or religious stage, except Kierkegaard's stage is not nearly so world-involved.

Schopenhauer, like all the German romanticists who followed Kant, was hostile to the scientific method and the concept of objectivity. In this he would alienate most American journalists today as they plunge ever more deeply into scientifically based "precision journalism" and retain their basic faith in journalistic objectivity. What good is Schopenhauer's mystical and emotional philosophy of intuition and will-lessness? the modern journalist would probably ask. Must not a journalist have a strong will in order to do the difficult job of providing facts and interpretation?

The romanticists, Schopenhauer included, believed that the source of knowledge is intuition, feeling, faith, or passion and that a person is an emotional rather than a rational being. They rejected the values of the Enlightenment, scorning Aristotelian logic, turning to subjectivism in order to plumb the realities of the inner world of feeling. Pessimism reigned; the world was basically in agony, and the only solution (for Schopenhauer) was to deny one's will and go into a kind of Nirvana-like oblivion. Other romanticists, such as Friedrich Nietzsche (1844–1900), would not deny the will but would exalt it, affirm it, and have it lead one to the transcendent level of the "Overman."

Many practitioners of today's journalism would find much of Schopenhauer's philosophy congenial and perhaps even helpful. They are the modern romantics, the dabblers in Eastern religions or in existentialism; they are the ones who would deny "objective journalism" and would try to find the Big Picture in subjective writing; they are the followers of the "New Journalism" of the 1960s exemplified by Norman Mailer, Gay Talese, and Tom Wolfe. But even for these journalistic types, Schopenhauer would be somewhat alien—too mystical, too divorced from certainty, too non-ideological, and too devoid of egoism.

But many journalists today are imbued with Schopenhauer's pessimism: They are prophets of doom, seeing our society disintegrating before our eyes; crime, racism, and intolerance increasing; revolutions and violence everywhere, even in our own backyards; and a growing cynicism that denies even that virtue is possible. Because the "sky is falling" for these potential followers of Schopenhauer, there seems to be only two things to do: take Nietzsche's path and willfully assert self and continue striving and competing, or sublimate the will, as Schopenhauer advises, and avoid the conflict.

Most journalists undoubtedly would find Nietzsche's path more inviting. The journalist who went too far down Schopenhauer's path would, of course, fall from the ranks of journalists completely or at least become content with providing audience members with personal intuitions, feelings, opinions, and impressions. Such subjective journalism is interesting and perhaps even enlightening in some instances. But if the mainstream of journalism becomes too clogged with such messages, the traditional concept of a news-oriented journalism will disappear, and a kind of nihilistic proliferation of impressionistic and propagandistic communication will result in a demise of fact-reporting and a credible base of reliable data.

But at least Schopenhauer, if we stop at his second stage of moral development in which the ego recognizes the importance of other egos, provides us with a kind of social consciousness that might be of use to the journalist. At one point Schopenhauer wrote that it was easy to preach morality but hard to give it a foundation. This is certainly true, and perhaps if we stop at his second stage of social awareness, we might say that it provides at least a framework for such a foundation.

It is Schopenhauer's final stage in which the journalist would in a sense sacrifice self on an altar of Nothingness, that his or her philosophy would be of no real use to the modern journalist who must be an active social participant and reporter. Schopenhauer's moral foundation seems to disappear in this final stage, where social concerns dissipate as one merges with everything and everybody. Even in a journalism that is like "the second hand on the clock of history," there must be a journalistic will—a will to achieve even a superficial reflection of history as it develops.

[15]

ALEXIS DE TOCQUEVILLE

Journalists wanting to get an "outside view" of the American press and a perceptive and incisive look at how democracy works in their country must be familiar with *Democracy in America,* published in France in 1835 and 1840. Its author, Alexis de Tocqueville (1805–1859) came to America in 1831, ostensibly to study the penal system, and traveled from New York to the limits of the country's western expansion and from Quebec to New Orleans. His main interest was democracy and how it worked in America.

The book, which became an immediate success and propelled Tocqueville to fame in Europe, contains keen insights into the foundations of American society, describes the tensions a capitalist democracy creates, and hints at problems that would arise from the American experience with democracy. It is considered perhaps the finest depiction of the spirit of American life and is one of the most often-quoted works in political theory. Tocqueville, on his trips, conversed with such figures as John Quincy Adams, Daniel Webster, Sam Houston, and President Andrew Jackson. And, as a person of keen observations and an analytical mind, his astute observations have earned him a lasting reputation.

Tocqueville was an aristocrat and was easily able to contrast his country's class-based society and that of the new democracy in the New World. He pointed out advantages of aristocracy and advantages of democracy in a surprisingly even-handed way, in itself a good example for the modern journalist. He did strike a note derived from Aristotle: that "as the condition of men becomes equal amongst a people, individuals seem of less, and society of greater importance." He warned of the possibility that one day every citizen will be assimilated and lost in the crowd and that nothing will remain but the "great and imposing image of the people at large."

Democracy tends toward the above direction, he wrote, but he raised the question (posed by Erich Fromm much later in his *Escape from Freedom*) of whether people really desire to be free to shape their own destinies, goals, and values. He did, in such a discussion, anticipate 20th-century writers who have written about "mass society," "the organization man," and "the lonely crowd."

Tocqueville was also getting at what later writers were to say about democracy: that, in representing majority opinion, the national government might well get too zealous and too effective and that minorities might be neglected. For Tocqueville, the danger lay in too much government, not in too little. And he, like many philosophers, recognized that majorities can be tyrannical. In this he was close to American conservatives of the 20th century. Although Tocqueville was critical of democracy, his analysis and suggestions were sympathetic, and he was convinced that Americans themselves would solve the problems of a free society.

In his first volume of *Democracy in America,* Tocqueville dealt with press freedom in the United States. He presented a good contrast of French and American newspapers, one that probably is as true today as in the 1800s. In France newspapers gave very limited space to advertising, whereas some three-quarters of the papers in America were filled with advertisements. In France the papers devoted great space to "passionate discussions," whereas American papers gave mainly "political intelligence and trivial anecdotes."

American newspapers, in Tocqueville's view, abused the powers of thought and serious intellectual concern. He saw them as consisting largely of coarse appeals to the passions and assaults on the character of individuals, invading their privacy and pointing out negative things about them. He says that people of esteem and authority in America are afraid to write in the newspapers (unlike in France), and they are thereby deprived of the "most powerful instrument which they can use to excite the passions of the multitude to their own advantage."

Personal opinions of American editors carry no weight with the American public, Tocqueville opined. What the public wants in a newspaper is factual knowledge, and the only way journalists can support their own views is by changing or distorting facts. Modern American journalists may certainly take exception to that observation, pointing out that this situation has changed significantly, with editorials, columns, letters, and op-ed pieces now having a high readership.

In the second volume of *Democracy in America,* Tocqueville took up the subject of the relationship between public associations and newspapers. He noted that newspapers are needed increasingly as people become more equal and individualism more to be feared. He saw newspapers as very important: they not only protect freedom, they maintain civilization. They are essential to public projects and associations; without them, he said, there would be no common activity. Newspapers, according to Tocqueville, bring people together and are needed to keep them united in common undertakings. As associations of people increase, the number of newspapers increases.

What about press freedom? Tocqueville was no great advocate. He saw it as mainly preventing evils, as being a kind of "watchdog on government," rather than noting anything positive that it might accomplish. Mostly he observed that American journalists used their freedom primarily to intrude into the private affairs of others, to accentuate the negative and the sensational rather than to educate the public in important matters or call the people to higher levels of public concern or morality.

Tocqueville, being an aristocrat in a democratic country, saw Americans as caring little for the outward form of human actions—manners. This was, to him, rather sad, for he saw manners as a reflection of character that gave human activities a kind of predictability and grace. Here he is reflecting the beliefs of Confucius, Aristotle, and Burke on the importance of habits and good manners. In democratic countries, Tocqueville noted, manners are devoid of dignity. Why is this? His answer may startle American journalists today: Because private life in democracies is "extremely petty" because of the fact that "the mind has few opportunities of rising above the engrossing cares of domestic interests."

According to Tocqueville, true dignity in manners comes from always taking one's proper station—neither too high nor too low. And manners, in aristocracies, can be found among peasants or among princes. But in democracies, all classes and stations are vague, and so manners, often full of arrogance, are lacking in dignity and are never well-trained or accomplished. The American journalist would probably reply to this: Amen, and bravo to that! In the democratic journalistic newsroom, for example, there is a flexible, informal, rather unpredictable camaraderie (a kind of absence of predictable manners) that manifests itself in a relatively equal treatment of editors, reporters, printers, and janitors. And it is considered a good thing, not a "lack of dignity."

Tocqueville chided the English for criticizing the Americans for not having manners; he said that the English (at least the middle class) exemplified the very thing they blamed in the United States. They did not realize that they were deriding themselves, to the great amusement of the French aristocracy, when they criticized the manners of Americans. One thing Tocqueville noted is that, although manners are not as uniform in America as in France, they are frequently more sincere.

What do manners have to do with ethics or virtue? Tocqueville said that, although they don't constitute virtue, they often embellish it. Acting according to manners causes every outward action to be dictated by "a natural elevation of thought and feeling, by delicacy and regularity of taste, and by urbanity." Such manners "throw a pleasing charm over human nature," and although the picture is often a false one, said Tocqueville, it cannot be viewed without satisfaction. And, what's more, acting with thoughtfulness and courtesy often brings inward and substantial change in the direction of true virtue and develops character.

Perhaps modern journalists can learn little of importance, in the way of philosophical insights, from Tocqueville. But they can at least savor his precise and astute reporting and analysis, and they can appreciate the directness and clarity of his language. Even in English translation it sparkles. They can also see that many of the weaknesses found in journalism today were spotted by a foreigner in the first half of the 19th century. In fact, the reader of *Democracy in America* will find that the well-known Hutchins Commission, which appraised the American press immediately after World War II, actually served as little more than an extended footnote to Alexis de Tocqueville.

[16]

JOHN STUART MILL

John Stuart Mill (1806–1873) is the best known of the 19th-century British philosophers called utilitarians. A defender of personal and political liberty and a social reformer, his essay *On Liberty* (1859) is one of the foremost declamations on freedom ever written. One of its leading statements sets the stage for libertarianism, which has dominated American journalism: "The only freedom which deserves the name, is that of pursuing our own good in our own way, so long as we do not attempt to deprive others of theirs, or impede their efforts to obtain it."

His grand principle of liberty was stated in other ways in the essay, but basically he restrains liberty only in the case of self-protection, when it might harm others, and when it might bring evil to others. The problem with this, of course, is that almost anything journalists do affects and may harm others; certainly this is true with the expression of opinions. Despite Mill's noble defense of freedom, we are still left with a vague idea of freedom's limits. This is why the debate rages on, libel suits are brought against journalists, and philosophers and others continue to try to define and explain the nature and scope of freedom.

Other than this rather short essay *On Liberty,* the most influential work of Mill was his *Utilitarianism,* published in 1861. In it he set out his ideas about the "greatest happiness of the greatest number" as a moral principle, which was to be known as the principle of utility. Mill had inherited this idea from Jeremy Bentham and Mill's own father, James, who in turn had been influenced by Hobbes and Hume and the French philosopher Helvétius. While retaining many of the basics of the old utilitarianism, Mill humanized the philosophy without destroying its basics.

In *Utilitarianism,* Mill provides a moral theory which holds that actions are right in proportion to the degree of happiness they bring. Every person's good is a happiness to that person, and the general happiness, it would follow for Mill, is a good for the entire society. This contention has received much criticism but has stood the test of time and remains the foundation for most of what we know as social ethics today.

Two varieties of utilitarianism are *act* utilitarianism and *rule* utilitarianism. Act utilitarianism says that, when trying to determine what is the right thing to do, one should ask which act will bring about the greatest happiness or good in that particular situation. There are no rules; everything is situational. But in rule utilitarianism, which stems from Mill, we make decisions according to rules that we believe will promote the greatest good for everyone. We ask not which act maximizes happiness or good, but which rule does. Actually, there is a third kind of utilitarianism lurking in a twilight zone between Jeremy Bentham and Kant—what might be called general utilitarianism. The question here is what would be the effect on the general social good if everyone were to do this particular thing in a case like this one. This propensity to universalize along with utility combines the ideas of Jeremy Bentham with those of Kant.

Utilitarianism is a kind of synthesis of Christianity and hedonism. The first urges a person to love his or her neighbor; the second, to love pleasure. In utilitarianism, if an action maximizes pleasure among people, then it is moral, and the theory says that a person's duty is to serve a quantitative standard of value. Service is not to the well-being of another person or even the nation but to the greatest happiness of the greatest number. As to one's own happiness, Mill would have the person be "disinterested" or "strictly impartial"; he would have individuals sublimate personal happiness to the happiness of the whole.

Mill wrestled with this quandary in his philosophy, his basic liberal individualism taking second place to his social utility principle that subordinated the individual to the collective. He had been justifying individual freedom by noting its contribution to the social welfare; he came to see this paradox and amended his political views, ending his life as a self-proclaimed "qualified socialist."

Most of the libertarian journalists today are perhaps also utilitarians, largely making their ethical decisions on the basis of perceived consequences that would bring happiness. Many of them, without realizing it, justify a free press by a kind of social utilitarian premise: society should permit the press to be free because a free press can best serve society's needs and interests.

This utilitarian rationale, unlike John Locke's "natural rights" reason for freedom, implies that the press can have its freedom as long as it serves society in a "responsible" manner. Unlike the press having a natural right to freedom, the press must earn freedom by conforming to the principle of utility. If we consider utilitarianism in this manner, then Mill does not come off as such a great stalwart of a free press; rather, what is most important to him is a good (or happy) society. Many people, of course, would not provide such an interpretation of Mill's utilitarianism.

At any rate, Mill was not as convinced of the absolute nature of free expression as was Locke. If such expression causes social harm, Mill believed, it should be circumscribed. Whereas Locke had seen press freedom as a God-given natural right, Mill saw it in utilitarian terms: what could it do in bringing about social good or happiness? But Mill definitely championed freedom.

In his famous essay *On Liberty,* he wrote: "If all mankind minus one were of one opinion, and only that person were of the contrary opinion, mankind would be no more justified in silencing that one person, than he, if he had the power, would be justified in silencing mankind." We might note, however, that Mill was talking about opinions and not about the mass of information mushrooming around us today. We do know that Mill valued free expression generally and counted it essential for good government. He even said that it was equal in value to good government because it was necessary for the existence of good government.

Mill felt that his freedom principle was appropriate only in societies of relatively high educational standards in which people could *rationally* exercise freedom. He did not project his freedom concept to everyone. For example, he would exclude from his freedom principle all "backward states of society." For such states, despotism would remain necessary until such time as social evolution would bring these people to the level of Western civilization. Freedom, for Mill, was for those who could use it for the betterment and happiness of society.

Despite limitations on freedom in Mill's philosophy, he believed, with Aristotle, that only through free expression could a person become truly human, fully actualized. He also contributed to modern journalism a great respect for message pluralism, purposive choice, close observation, careful thought, and unambivalent writing. Mill thought that truth could be suppressed for a while but never killed; it may be extinguished many times, but it will finally be rediscovered and brought to light. He disagreed with John Milton's famous self-righting principle that Truth will always win out in a free encounter with Falsehood. He called that "one of those pleasant falsehoods" that will not hold up in reality. What he proclaimed was the *indestructibility* of truth, not its superiority in a fight with falsehood.

So the modern journalist can learn many things from Mill. One is that others must be considered—their happiness, their good, their welfare. Another: free expression leads to the general good by providing more avenues for action. Still another is that knowledge is never complete, and constant effort is needed to obtain it. Yet another is that human potential cannot be reached without freedom to choose, to express opinions, and to associate freely with whomever one desires. And, says Mill, indestructible truth is waiting to be discovered.

[17]

SØREN KIERKEGAARD

Søren Kierkegaard (1813–1855) provides an individualistic, existential foundation for the journalist's philosophy. His basic perspective was also passionately Christian, although he was contemptuous of organized religion and any kind of doctrine that minimized individual decision making and personal existence.

Usually considered a forerunner, along with Nietzsche, of 20th-century existentialism, Kierkegaard's philosophy attacked the rational humanism of his day and urged a personal commitment, a "leap of faith" fueled by passion and feeling, which he saw as being as important as reason and intellect in the essential meaning and value of a person's life. Kierkegaard defended the sovereignty of the individual against the conformity of mass-mindedness. He was especially contemptuous of the Hegelian notion that the significance of the individual comes from his or her participation in the collective.

Probably most important for the journalist would be the Danish thinker's *Fear and Trembling* (1843), *Either/Or* (1843), *Stages on Life's Way* (1845), and *Judge for Yourselves* (1851). Kierkegaard's existentialism (at least in core concepts) is similar to later French existentialists such as Gabriel Marcel, Albert Camus, and Jean-Paul Sartre. All stressed the importance of personal and genuine choice. The Kierkegaardian journalist, for example, would choose not by using pre-existing criteria and principles but within an atmosphere of doubt and uncertainty. Such non-directed choices (coming from outside sources) are the real existential ones and are made by a leap of faith that affirms the existence of God. Such a choice or leap of faith must be made without the advice of others, must be made in "fear and trembling," relying on nothing other than oneself.

A collateral idea to this personal choosing is Kierkegaard's insistence that one take personal responsibility for his or her actions. Making these personal leaps of faith often results in consequences, not always good, and a person must be willing to live with this responsibility. No place exists in Kierkegaard's philosophy for a journalist shifting the blame for an action to someone else—an editor or publisher, for example. When the journalist acts, the buck stops with him or her.

Four of Kierkegaard's basic tenets or emphases, all certainly important to many journalists, are the importance of freedom, commitment, action, and responsibility. These would provide the basis for an existentialist journalism. The Kierkegaardian journalist would be a person who is impassioned (committed), interested in personal growth through choosing, oriented toward possibilities, uneasy with passivity and unconcern; he or she would prize freedom and authenticity, extol individualism and be intolerant of conformity, basically be a subjectivist and not an objectivist in epistemology, and constantly be developing, changing, and creating self through commitment and action.

One of the earliest thinkers to suggest a developmental model for moral growth (see *Stages on Life's Way*), Kierkegaard saw a person going through three stages. First, and the lowest and most elemental, is what he called the *aesthetic stage*—a prerational, youthful, restless, energetic stage of the "sensuous immediate." This early stage is dominated by "self-love" and instinctual preferences and dislikes. Right and wrong, at this stage, are determined mainly by feelings and intuition.

The life of the aesthete (not limited to the artistic) is a life that lacks continuity, with nothing to hold it together, always seeking some gratification. It lusts for enjoyment and abhors the idea of commitment to any person or thing. In addition, it is life based on the accidental, depending largely on the accident of possessing some endowment, such as intelligence, athletic ability, or good looks. It is also a life that judges things on the basis of interest. The aesthete cares not whether something or somebody is good or bad, but rather whether they are interesting or uninteresting. The aesthetic life seeks to be entertained, excited, and thrilled. And finally, the aesthetic life is concerned with external matters rather than internal essence. At this aesthetic level, Kierkegaard sees people trying to manipulate their environment rather than change themselves, not understanding that life's success depends on what goes on within themselves.

At this initial stage a person pursues a range of pleasures but cannot escape boredom and troubles. The peace and personal happiness that a person seeks are not forthcoming. Despair is the result and, in many cases, eventually motivates a person to seek a dedication to duty, obedience, and the guidelines of an objective morality.

At this point a person moves to Kierkegaard's second (and higher) stage, which he called the *ethical stage.* Here one seeks guidance for ethical action and moves from self-interest to a more altruistic position. Rationality is enthroned, with life acquiring a certain unity and coherence. A person is now concerned largely with social obligations and public-mindedness, with fulfilling obligations. At this stage life becomes significant, not just interesting or uninteresting. And the person seeking good, the right, and the valuable is acting significantly. Life is no longer simply a series of momentary excitements; it has a continuity that gives it direction.

The ethical person has learned three important life secrets, says Kierkegaard: (1) that resignation to obligations and claims is needed for a person to discover oneself, (2) that each day of faithfulness (commitment) to ethical standards increases a sense of well-being and achievement, and (3) that the world is filled with drama due to the conflict between good and evil and that one's striving for the good must be without ceasing.

However, according to Kierkegaard, a person may eventually find this rational (ethical) stage too cold and formalistic, too reason-oriented and too much concerned with justification for every action. So at this point a person moves to the third and final of Kierkegaard's stages—the stage of *religion* or *faith.*

Here again at this highest stage a person relies on feeling, believing, sensation, emotion, and intuition. Similar to the first stage in its non-rational emphasis, this religious or faith stage, however, is not self-centered. Instead, it is God-centered. As a person comes to this final developmental stage, he or she realizes personal weaknesses, recognizing that reason has failed to clarify things or bring contentment. So a person comes to this ultimate stage where there is a merging with the Absolute (understood as God).

Making personal choices—leaps of faith—and making them continually: this is the core meaning of the religious (faith) stage. A person does not exist, believed Kierkegaard, until he or she acts from faith rather than from some outside formula or system promising moral results. This faith in God does not "compel" a person to make ethical choices (the person may not); rather, it energizes a person to scorn an objective ethics and to construct his or her own ethical life. Thereupon one's own individual existence is validated.

For Kierkegaard, as for Christian ethicists generally, love is the cornerstone of ethics—a religious love (*agape*) that is distinguished from all other kinds. The reason: the source is God. Like a hidden spring, we cannot see the source, but we discover it through faith. We love God and, necessarily, we love others. Ethics, then, is channeled in the right direction by this kind of love. It is not like human love, which changes and can become jealous or possessive or can fade and pass away. The love that stems from God does not change; it endures; it bears all things and never fails. It cares about others and wants to do good to them, not because they manifest lovable traits but simply because *agape* requires it. It is love universalized and undifferentiated.

So for Kierkegaard, Christian love rises above the ethical level that is concerned primarily with obligations. It is not a love directed at some people only. There is no obligation to love; there is simply the God-directed impulse to do so. This, then, for Kierkegaard and most Christian ethicists, is the moving force of morality and the stimulus that motivates the highest level of ethical activity.

We can see that Kierkegaard's three-stage model rises from

a duty to self, to a duty to others, and to a duty to God and could be described as a progression from body to mind to heart. The Danish philosopher (he preferred being called a religious writer) did not think, of course, that everybody went through all of these stages. Many would never get past the first stage; others would progress to and be stuck in the second one. Only a much smaller group would reach the third and highest (for Kierkegaard) level of faith.

Kierkegaard was not much interested in epistemology, but he did have something to say about objective and subjective truth. He recognized the commonly held idea of "objectivity" as being associated with Kant's "disinterested judge." Many thinkers held the idea that there was, indeed, impartial, dispassionate truth—a kind of objective truth. This, of course, is what many of today's journalists think of when they talk of objective journalism or reporting. And for them, such journalism is good; it is what journalism should be.

Kierkegaard would have none of this kind of objectivity. For him, such terms as disinterested and dispassionate were pejorative. Such a goal of objectivity was nothing but an impossible ideal. Kierkegaard believed that there is no such thing as an impartial observer. All truth is filtered through the mental, emotional, valuative, and psychological strainer of the individual person. For Kierkegaard, one simply could not step outside oneself, and what is more, any attempt to adopt such a neutral and disinterested posture would be inauthentic and even destructive to one's personhood.

Far ahead of his time, Kierkegaard anticipated some of the main views of today's postmodernism. For example, like the French postmodernist Foucault, he recognized that so-called dispassionate reason and objectivity are greatly affected by personal values and interests. It may well be that because Kierkegaard had such an individualist and personal attitude toward communication his philosophy is generally considered among the most readable in philosophical literature.

The concept of impartiality, like objectivity, is a concept of interest for the journalist, and so it was for Kierkegaard. The journalist who aspires to be impartial is certainly being partial to impartiality. And, for Kierkegaard, the pursuit of impartiality, like its subsuming concept, objectivity, is not only impossible but unfortunate. Such a pursuit draws us away from our real selves, from espousing our real concerns, beliefs, and opinions. It keeps us from fully exercising our powers of interpretation and critical abilities. And it serves as a kind of escapist mechanism keeping a person from the anguish (and personal growth) of making decisions.

Subjectivity, on the other hand, posed no problem for Kierkegaard. It was in this inward, personal (subjective) sense that he believed one best developed toward a meaningful personhood. Such a belief was still not popular in Kierkegaard's day. The influence of the French philosopher René Descartes (1596–1650), who condemned the imagination and passions as barriers to truth, was still strong, and philosophers generally were bound by this more scientific stance.

So certainly Kierkegaard would disdain the modern attempt to produce objective journalism. He would cry out for more subjectivity in journalism, more personal involvement, more journalistic stand-taking, more choosing, more action, and more acceptance of personal responsibility. He would also scorn any type of conformity within various journalistic media, or even conformity among them. He might even decry the whole idea of "mass" communication, for he saw a loss of personal integrity and growth in the growing trend toward institutional depersonalization.

In our modern world in which social adjustment and public-mindedness hold sway, it is interesting to be reintroduced to a person like Kierkegaard (and even Nietzsche) who emphasized self-enhancement, inwardness, and subjectivity and taught that becoming a fully developed self is more important than worrying about one's relationship to the environment and place in the social structure.

[18]

KARL MARX

With the possible exception of John Stuart Mill, Karl Marx (1818–1883) has had the greatest impact on 20th-century journalism and journalistic thinking of any 19th-century thinker. Unlike Mill and other more individualistic liberal thinkers, however, Marx saw social needs as taking precedence over the basic Enlightenment brand of libertarianism. So he was ready to support a journalistic system geared to being an instrument for social progress (for him, bringing down capitalism and enthroning a dictatorship of the working class). And for Marx, such a journalistic libertarianism as envisioned by Mill would have to be postponed for awhile—until the advent of the final utopian communist world.

Marx differed from Mill chiefly in that he believed the ultimate goal of a person was to achieve the good of society, whereas Mill placed more emphasis on exalting the individual. Journalists who now see the excesses and even horrors of the so-called Marxist system of the former Soviet Union should be warned that Marx himself would not have approved of much that went on from the time of Lenin, and certainly Stalin, until the beginning of the final decade of the 20th century. The basically humanistic and statist philosophy of Marx (especially of the early Marx) has been distorted in many respects by a series of ideological leaders in countries such as the Soviet Union, China, and Cuba. Just as Christianity cannot be judged by excesses committed in its name, the Marxist concept of communism cannot be judged by the authoritarianism and criminality of its later disciples and adherents.

Karl Marx was born in the Rhineland town of Trier of wealthy Jewish parents who converted to Christianity when Marx was a child. He studied for a time at the University of

Bonn and later at the University of Berlin where he was influenced by the thought of Hegel, who had taught there and had recently died. Marx was especially impressed by Hegel's dialectical analysis. And like Hegel, Marx was interested in this developmental concept and the related philosophy of history. As Hegel had been, Marx was also responsive to the concept of personal alienation. But Marx, unlike Hegel, was a proponent of quick social "fixes," of radical revolutionary solutions, and this made him unpopular and generally unsuitable for the disciplined world of German university teaching. So he decided to spread his ideas via journalism.

For some five months he edited the *Rheinische Zeitung* until it was suppressed by the Prussian government. In 1843, Marx and his wife left for Paris where he wrote for a revolutionary publication until it, too, was shut down. In France he began his friendship and collaboration with Friedrich Engels, a like-minded anti-capitalist. On a trip to London in 1847 to attend a meeting of the newly formed Communist League, he and Engels were asked to write a simple statement of the League's doctrine. This resulted in the *Communist Manifesto,* published in 1848.

The next year Marx, in political disrepute in Germany, France, and Belgium, moved his family to London where he lived for the rest of his life. Marx struggled in these early days to support himself and his family, mainly by writing articles. He also kept busy by participating in many political debates and controversies and working on his book *Das Kapital,* a criticism of capitalism.

While in his 50s, Marx gained some notoriety; *Das Kapital* was being widely read, and he enjoyed many associations with like-minded theorists all over Europe. However, his last years were unhappy; he suffered through several deaths within his family and died himself in 1883. Engels delivered the funeral address. He stressed how Marx's mission in life was to contribute to the overthrow of capitalist society and the liberation of the proletariat from exploitation by the bourgeoisie, and how he was revered and mourned by millions "of revolutionary fellow workers" throughout the world.

It is ironic that Marx is so closely identified with the proletariat and that Engels would talk of him as a "worker" when he was the son of a lawyer, was university educated, and spent his time as a theorist, speaker, and writer.

Engels himself was the son of a wealthy cotton-spinner. Neither was a proletarian. Certain questions have been asked (for instance, by the British philosopher Karl Popper in *The Open Society and its Enemies,* London: Routledge, 1945, p. 194) as to how Marx and Engels could formulate a proletarian ideology that proletarians had not been able to formulate for themselves. And if they could escape *their* "class" ideology and enter the ranks of the proletariat, then why not urge a similar large-scale movement through education and persuasion, rather than violent revolution? Would this not be a more humane resolution than going through a dismantling and reorganization of society?

Perhaps not, the impatient Marx would say. And such questions are too philosophical, Marx might add. For he and Engels were abandoning philosophy and replacing it with what they called scientific socialism. Still, Marx's "scientific" concept drew heavily on the philosophical ideas of Hegel, especially that part relating to historical development. Marx substituted a materialistic dialectic (changes in modes of production and exchange) for Hegel's spiritual, or idealistic, dialectic of consciousness development. Whereas Hegel thought ideas moved the world, Marx felt that matter or materialism was the moving force of history.

For Hegel the basic paradigm for change was gradual and natural, certainly evolutionary, although he recognized that some revolutionary change could be effected by such "world historical" figures as Napoleon, Frederick the Great, or Attila the Hun. Marx, on the other hand, saw change as revolutionary, involving the destruction of one class by another—the bourgeoisie by the proletariat. In this cataclysmic view of change, Marx was much closer to such thinkers as Nietzsche and the survival-of-the-fittest advocates than to the Enlightenment thinkers and the rationalism they exemplified.

Although Marx and Engels liked to call their system scientific, many critics deny any scientific base for their pronouncements. For example, the British historian Paul Johnson in his *Intellectuals* (New York: Harper & Row, 1988, p. 69) proposes that Marx did not understand capitalism because he was unscientific. Johnson maintains that in Marx's writings (especially in *Das Kapital*) he evidenced a disregard for truth "which at times amounts to contempt." That is why, says Johnson, Marxism as a system cannot produce its intended results, and to call it scientific is preposterous.

So far as Marx's ethical theory is concerned, it might be called a form of moral positivism, stating that the moral standard is simply the one that exists. But it goes beyond the normal moral positivism which would postulate that "might is right." Marx's version is futuristic, saying that the coming might (the state of communism) is right.

Just how journalism and the press would fit into this ideal world of the future we aren't sure. Marx never gives us a view of such a press reality. He did deal with the press in the revolutionary and intervening period on the road to communism. He saw it as an important instrument in the hands of the rising working classes, aiding in education and as an agitator and propagandist for change and revolution. He saw the press, at least when he was writing in English for such newspapers as the *New York Journal,* as a searcher for truth. At that time he saw journalism as needed to aid free inquiry, and he viewed censorship as socially harmful.

Libertarian though the above may sound, it is doubtful that Marx held such beliefs throughout his life. He later made it clear that a communist press would function basically to perpetuate and expand the socialist system and that the transmission of social policy, not digging for objective truth, would be the main reason for the existence of a communist media system. Mass media, under such a system, would be instruments of government and the Communist Party. They would be owned by the State (the people) and directed by the Party or its functionaries. Criticism would be permitted, but not of basic ideology. Marx noted that in the Marxist revolution, the mass media, along with individual people, would have to sublimate themselves to the State.

The ethical journalist, then, in Marx's view, is the person who is loyal to the communist system. Loyalty is equated with ethical behavior. Whatever the journalist or a mass medium does to contribute to communism or the Socialist State and Party is moral; whatever is done to harm or hinder the State or the growth of communism is immoral. One could say that Marx would still see in this a journalistic concern for truth, because truth would be a pragmatic or useful truth—useful to the "people's democracy" or the communist system. Certainly Marx would see the capitalist press concept of freedom as inherently irresponsible. For instance, he would note that the capitalist press undermines social decorum and decency with its cheap and vulgar content and advertising; that it keeps the workers from recognizing how they are exploited; and that it exists solely as an instrument of the ruling class (the bourgeoisie) as it receives special status and privilege for its help in social control and the perpetuation of the status quo.

Marx saw his socialist press, undeniably controlled by the State-Party apparatus, as existing in a transitional or temporary phase of history. When the State and its organizations and bureaucracies "withered away" in the last days, a pristine communist society of cooperating and classless people would result. And presumably, in those days the press would indeed be free: free from any need of outside direction; free to be autonomous in the sense of being of the people, by the people, and for the people. So it is understandable that in the former Soviet Union the press was seen as an instrument to be used by the State and Party. It was not Marx's intention that such press control would be permanent. Marx, it might be said, was a "futuristic libertarian" and saw the need for temporary authoritarianism en route to his communist utopia.

Such a press philosophy is consistent with Marx's overriding dialectical vision of society. Marx proposed in his historical analysis that the ultimate synthesis in his dialectic would be communism, the last and utopian stage of history, after socialism (the antithesis) had clashed with capitalism (the thesis) and had overcome it. Nobody at that point would control productive means, class struggle would have ended, and all bourgeois institutions would have withered away. Marx makes such existence sound idyllic: society regulating production; people doing one thing today and another tomorrow, hunting in the morning and fishing in the afternoon, raising cattle in the evening and criticizing and discussing after dinner. His lasting ideal was that one would have the freedom to become a full human being, with sufficient material goods for a happy life and an existence leading to the free use of full physical and mental faculties.

Marx had a lot to say about freedom. Communist freedom would be the opposite of the alienation that results mainly from economic exploitation. Marxian freedom would be freedom from being treated by others as an object—freedom to become one's own creator by and through free choices. A kind of existentialist stance? Perhaps. Marx stressed subjectivity, self-consciousness, and freedom; he emphasized the *making* of the human person by his or her own choices. This Marxian concern for subjectivity as a human and social goal was consistent with the general European romanticism of the time, even with those hostile to Marxism in its more radical elements.

The concept of freedom, accepted by socialist societies that have been spawned by Marx's thought, has mainly been a people's freedom from having to make traumatic economic and social decisions, freedom to support the system, and freedom to find and correct flaws in the working of the system. This same kind of freedom has applied to the press also: freedom to protect the people from capitalist exploitation, to keep them on the road to communism, and to solidify and enlarge socialist ideology. Certainly this kind of neo-Marxist freedom is alien to capitalist societies, in which freedom is associated with maximum personal and press autonomy and lack of editorial control by non-press entities.

Modern American journalists, steeped in the concept of the press and government as adversaries, would also find the Marxist "supportive" conception of journalistic ethics strange, if not outright ridiculous. Can you imagine many American journalists saying: If I support the government, I'm ethical; if I don't, I'm unethical? But again, perhaps this is the main difference between John Stuart Mill, the individualist, and Karl Marx, the collectivist; although they both wanted a better society, the first stressed pluralistic personal effort, and the second emphasized cooperative or collective effort. The Millians of modern journalism put their faith in contentiousness and social friction; the Marxists of modern journalism extol cooperation, group solidarity, and social harmony.

Regardless of Marx's now-discredited economic ideas and his perhaps unrealistic faith in a human desire for state parentalism, his legacy to journalistic thinking has been considerable. His criticisms of the vulgarities of a capitalist society are largely valid, although his idea of a dualistic capitalist world of workers and exploiters is simplistic and does not conform to the realities and complexities of capitalist societies since his death. His ideas of the myth of objectivity have largely been accepted in journalism. His humanistic inclinations—concern for the poor and the underdog, for instance—which he showed especially in his early years, are good models for modern journalists.

Just as there are important things to be learned from collectivists or statists such as Hobbes, Rousseau, and Hegel, journalists can benefit from similar ideas gleaned from Karl Marx. A communitarian perspective in journalism, growing in popularity at the end of the 20th century, owes much to Marx, especially the young Marx of his more humanistic years. For example, journalists would do well to share Marx's desire to see a world free from exploitation, poverty, misery, fear, and oppression. It may well be that, although his solution to many of the world's problems was over-idealistic and perhaps faulty, Marx set an example for the modern journalist who would desire to make at least a small part of the world a better place.

[19]

ALFRED KORZYBSKI

Journalists who want to depict the reality of the world in its multidimensional complexity and to have a more sophisticated view of language should turn to Alfred Korzybski (1879–1950) and his general semantics orientation. Such a perspective emphasizes the need for language usage that seeks to be more realistic and scientific, more sensitive to ways words affect thought and thought affects action. It is an orientation, said Korzybski, that gives more attention to making better linguistic maps of the territory of reality.

Korzybski, a Polish aristocrat, came to the United States just after World War I. Although trained as an engineer, he had a broad-ranging intellectual background and was later to use this eclecticism in his development of general semantics. He served in the Russian army during World War I and in various military capacities in Canada and the United States after the war. After his first book *Manhood of Humanity* (1921) came out, he decided to remain in the United States, developing his ideas related to general semantics that he had been refining for many years. This interest resulted in his classic tome on the orientation called *Science and Sanity*, published in 1933.

He taught his new general semantics at various venues, including a stint off campus at the University of Chicago (academicians largely were suspicious of this subject and were slow to work it into their curricula). In 1938, Korzybski founded the Institute of General Semantics in Darien, Connecticut, which served as the center for training and research in his work. People came from across the country and around the world to study with him. He directed seminars there, lectured widely, and wrote voluminously until his death in 1950.

Korzybski stressed a scientific language—at least he urged a scientific use of language. The old Western two-valued, unscientific use of language was harmful to interpersonal and international relationships. This either/or kind of language, which he traced back to Aristotle, should be replaced by a more "realistic" and "dynamic" orientation. And so he developed his system of general semantics, which he and his disciples referred to as "multivalued" or "non-Aristotelian."

This new system or orientation, according to Korzybski, stresses the dynamics of the real world and the basically static nature of language. Flux is an important aspect of general semantics: the need to use language so as best to depict the constant changes occurring in reality. Korzybski went back to the pre-Socratic Greek philosopher Heraclitus to make this point. Heraclitus had said something like this: No person steps in the same river twice. The river is constantly becoming a new river, and also, the person is constantly becoming a new person. Every time such a person steps, the person has changed, and the river has changed. All is new, although the old names prevail. So as Korzybski would put it, people should be aware of this weakness of language to keep up with reality: Bill Smith in 1970 is not Bill Smith in 1990; the Rhine River in 1990 is not the Rhine River in 1994.

Also very important to general semanticists is the idea that "the map is not the territory," that one must look at the substance behind the label and not be led astray by the names people and institutions carry. What a journalist, then, should do is to be a better "mapmaker." Maps may not be the territory, but there are better and worse maps. And since the journalist knows this and is in the linguistic mapmaking business, he or she should try to make maps that conform as closely to the reality of the territory as possible.

Also of great importance to Korzybski was the breaking down of stereotypes by recognizing that members of the same group (religion, race, political party) are really different and distinct. Arab 1 is not Arab 2; cow 1 is not cow 2, Korzybski would say. Certainly these emphasizes have great value for the journalist.

General semantics is a complex system that teaches that language can tyrannize or enslave us. Such mid–20th century writers and teachers as Stuart Chase, Wendell Johnson, and S. I. Hayakawa (in such books as *The Power of Words, People in Quandaries,* and *Language in Thought and Action*) have emphasized the power that language has over our thoughts and actions. Korzybski and his followers have tried to sensitize people to the potency of language and help them use words with more precision and sophistication.

Let us look briefly at the basic principles of general semantics, all of which can be usefully adapted to the field of journalism. (1) No two events in nature are identical; every event is unique. (2) Events flow into one another, making nature all of a piece, although language tends to classify nature into separate categories. (3) Nature exists in dynamic processes, but language is incapable of reflecting this. (4) Events, things, and people have unlimited characteristics that cannot be reflected in language. (5) Multivalued logic is essential to understanding and describing reality, but language tends to cast everything in extremes, such as liberal/conservative, good/bad, short/tall, black/white. (6) The word or symbol is not its referent; "the map is not the territory"; a name is not the essence of the named. (7) Language, which is basically static, tries to describe a world in process or flux. (8) Members of a group are different, and stereotypes need to be broken down. (9) Meanings are in people's heads, not in dictionaries; what a person who is using a word (encoding or decoding) means by that word is what is important, not what somebody else says the word means. (10) It is impossible to say everything about anything (the concept of "etc."). (11) When all verbalizing is over, there are always undefined terms. (12) Shy away from abstract terms when possible (such as moderate, loyal, beautiful), and when you must use them, illustrate what you mean by them.

Korzybskian semantics forces a journalist to think of completeness and balance in a story, and probably more important, the changing nature of people, places, and events. For at the core of general semantics is the idea of a "process" world in which all is *becoming,* in which the static verb "is" (of identity) normally distorts reality. Korzybski would have journalists be concerned with change and how language can best depict it.

This concern in general semantics with the world in process is similar to the Buddhist *samtana* (the idea of constant change, or arising and disappearing) and the concept of impermanence (*anicca*), of constant creation and destruction. Everything is changing, merging: This is the core message in Korzybskian semantics and Buddhism. The general semanticist would have the journalist try to describe this process or take it into consideration in the story process, whereas the Buddhist would probably consider it impossible and unrealistic even to try to depict it verbally.

The intellectual legacy of general semantics is great. And for the journalist, it is very important because communication of reality is at the core of a journalist's job. For the general semanticist, as it should be for the journalist, the world is of one piece, parts flowing and merging. This holistic concept, along with the idea of constant flux, lies at the foundation of modern journalism.

[20]

ROBERT MAYNARD HUTCHINS

Although Robert Maynard Hutchins (1899–1977) was not a journalist, his thought has made a deep impression in the development of journalistic philosophy since the mid-20th century. He and the 12 members of the Commission on Freedom of the Press (better known as the Hutchins Commission) who studied the American press at the end of World War II were responsible for a paradigm shift in press philosophy from an emphasis on press freedom to one that enthroned press responsibility. The whole theory of social responsibility of the press is usually traced back to the Hutchins Commission.

Despite the influence of his Commission report, very little has been written about Hutchins himself and his views of the press. Much, however, has been written about him as educator and moralist. He wrote very little about the press per se, but he spoke enthusiastically about journalism when asked, although he never developed his ideas systematically. So it is primarily through the report of the Commission (*A Free and Responsible Press*), published by the University of Chicago Press in 1947, that we get the best idea of Hutchins' thinking about journalism.

It was Henry Luce, publisher of *Life* and *Time* magazines, who had the idea of a commission to assess press performance in the United States. He pledged $200,000 and the *Encyclopedia Britannica* gave another $15,000 for the two-year study; Luce selected his old Yale friend Hutchins to chair it, after Judge Learned Hand turned down the offer. The University of Chicago, where Hutchins was chancellor, administered the funds but had no say as to how the money was spent. Hutchins chose the Commission members, intellectual friends of his who were ideologically compatible.

Hutchins manifested a great interest in press freedom and seemed not to see the danger that some of the Commission's recommendations could pose to such freedom. Literacy, he believed, was not enough to assure freedom (seemingly contradicting Jefferson); one had to be educated, and the best way to be educated, in his view, was to read the "great books." He maintained (in his popular *Education for Freedom* in 1944) that it was obvious that if everybody could read and all they read would be pulp magazines, obscene literature, and Hitler's *Mein Kampf,* the nation would be in deep trouble.

Freedom was always at the core of Hutchins' comments on the press, even when he was suggesting his own brand of guidance for the journalist. He was a firm supporter of what is called positive freedom, the kind we want *for* the sake of doing something that cannot be done unless we are free. Although he showed more interest in press freedom *for,* he also prized "negative freedom," or freedom *from* external control. He stressed the importance of press freedom as a means of making a contribution "to the maintenance and development of a free society." One might say that Hutchins interpreted press freedom as utilitarian: The press should be free to pursue high ideas, enlightenment, and morality so that society as a whole will be better. The press has rights only as they relate to doing social good, he believed. In a 1947 University of Chicago Round Table radio broadcast, he stressed press freedom but bemoaned journalism's inadequate service to society's needs and many deplorable press practices; he concluded that society will inevitably seek controls on the media, saying that "if the press is to preserve its liberty, it must be responsible or we will suddenly find that forces in society, perhaps the government, will deprive it of its liberty." His warning was no consolation to the press.

Hutchins was a Platonist in the sense that he wanted each medium to subordinate itself to the good of U.S. society as a whole. Today he would probably be called a communitarian, a term that developed during the final stage of Soviet communism and that today is used by those who see themselves as advocates of social responsibility—with a stress on taking care of one another, protecting the rights of the disadvantaged and the so-called underclasses of society. Communitarians are more interested in responsibilities than in rights. So Hutchins' emphasis on journalistic responsibility, rather than on journalistic freedom, is compatible with communitarianism.

Actually, only the term communitarian is new; various philosophers through the ages have stressed responsibility over rights and society's interest over the individual's interest. But it was probably Hutchins who ushered into the mid-20th century the emphasis behind the term, with his strong advocacy of press responsibility and the concomitant reduction of journalistic freedom. Actually, Hutchins never quite got around to suggesting overt censorship by government, but he implied that something of the sort might have to be done if the press failed to respond to the needs of society. He did suggest the possibility that the government might have to get into the communication business, if for nothing else than to provide another perspective. Hutchins seemed to think that the press can be whipped into shape by strong and intelligent external criticism, and his Commission even suggested an independent agency that would annually appraise the press. He also believed that media should criticize one another and that citizens should criticize the press.

Believing that the press (as well as formal education) has the responsibility to solve society's grave problems, Hutchins would recommend that journalists get an especially strong foundation in history and philosophy. Without these two fields, together with other disciplines needed to understand them, he believed journalists would be unable to helpfully criticize social institutions. He emphasized a liberal arts education and distrusted the social sciences. Recognizing that many people could not attend a university or would stop learning after graduation, he thought that the press has the responsibility to provide a basic and continuing education for society.

A humanist primarily, Hutchins (and his commissioners) seemed to have little trust in the scientific method, and this perhaps led to the non-methodological "study" of the press from 1944 to 1946. The Hutchins Commission interviewed only 58 people; staff members conducted about 200 other interviews. There was no systematic, methodological pattern to the study, and the conclusions reflected what the commissioners had already written in pre-study days. None of the commissioners was a journalist, and Commission meetings were not open to the public. Even Henry Luce felt the study was superficial and flawed.

Hutchins and his Commission set up high standards for the press, saying that if the press did not fulfill these standards it was irresponsible, and then proceeded to pass judgment on the press. The Commission found that, by and large, the American press was not responsible, that it was too concerned with its freedom and gave little or no attention to its social responsibilities. It dealt in too much trivia, negativism, sensationalism, and gossip. It was too sensitive to criticism and too engrossed in making a profit. It did not give the constituent groups in society proper exposure, and it did not provide significant information in a meaningful context. Basically, the Commission found the press too inward-looking, superficial, sensational, and greedy. And it passed its judgment: The American press was not socially responsible.

The Hutchins Commission made recommendations for the press: more external criticism and self-criticism, more continuing education for journalists, more attention to press ethics, more emphasis on complaints from the public. Hutchins was disappointed nearly a decade after the 1947 report came out that the press had not noticeably changed. He was angry that the media were still not criticizing each other and that outside criticism was met with hostility and an appeal to the First Amendment.

Not surprisingly, Hutchins never had anything good to say about journalism education. He was, in fact, not a friend of any trade schooling being a part of a university, and he thought of journalism education as just that. What journalists needed was a good liberal arts education, with special emphasis in philosophy and history. What journalists needed, according to Hutchins, was a good acquaintance with the wisdom of the great books, the classics of Western Civilization.

If Hutchins were looking at American newspapers today, he would probably be disappointed that they are not more "responsible." But journalists are more sensitive to their social responsibilities than they were at the end of World War II, and they have muted their cries of "press freedom" somewhat as they think increasingly about ethics and the effect of their activities. Much of what they accept as perfectly reasonable for them to do today is very close to what the Hutchins Commission recommended back in 1947.

[21]

ERIC HOFFER

Born in New York City, blind from age 7 to 15, educated in the School of Hard Knocks in the fields and ports of America, stamped with eclectic knowledge from a lifetime of voracious serious reading, Eric Hoffer (1902–1983) has a lot of wisdom to impart to journalists. No product of a formal university education, Hoffer launched his education at the age of 5 by teaching himself to read in both German and English.

Inexplicably, when he was 7, Hoffer lost his eyesight. As suddenly as he lost it, when he was 15 he could see again. He started to read 10 or 12 hours a day, believing that he might become blind again. For the next three years he proceeded to read almost every book in a secondhand bookstore near his home. After his father died in 1920, Hoffer bought a bus ticket to California where he rented a cheap room near the Los Angeles Central Library. He soon got a series of temporary jobs—washing dishes, loading pipe, moving furniture, raking leaves, and doing other work just to be able to eat.

He left Los Angeles at the end of the 1920s and moved to Anaheim, where while reading Goethe he came across a passage that served as an inspiration to him for the rest of his life: *Mut verloren—alles verloren,* meaning "Courage lost, all is lost." For the next decade Hoffer drifted all over California as a farm worker, reading in every free moment, discovering the great thinkers of history. And he was teaching himself to write, filling notebooks with thoughts gleaned from the various books he read.

Turned down for the armed services in 1941 because of health reasons, Hoffer became a longshoreman and began working regularly in 1942. He was 40 years old. He continued reading and writing in his notebooks; the men he worked with called him Professor. He was accumulating thoughts for his books to come, especially his best-known, *The True Believer.* French writers seemed to fascinate him most—Bergson, Pascal, Renan, Tocqueville, and Montaigne. He liked Dostoevsky and Jacob Burckhardt but said he got little from Plato or the German writers, who were generally abstruse, with the possible exceptions of Nietzsche and Heine.

The True Believer was published in 1951 and was a success. Its aphoristic style and wit, its insightful parallels, and its general wisdom were praised by almost all reviewers. Although he made considerable money from the book, Hoffer remained in his rough neighborhood on McAllister Street in San Francisco, and he continued his work on the waterfront. He also continued to write and published such volumes as *The Passionate State of Mind* (1955), *The Ordeal of Change* (1963), and *The Temper of Our Time* (1967). But it was *The True Believer* for which he is mainly remembered, and it is this book that has most to say to the journalist.

Translated into at least a dozen languages and selling more than a half a million copies in its first 10 years, *The True Believer* became required reading in many college and university classes. It largely propelled Hoffer into the public eye. He appeared on many radio and television shows, and his series of interviews with Eric Severeid (the first in 1967) made him a celebrity. He was even invited to the White House by Lyndon Johnson, a president he much respected. Hoffer formally retired in 1967, and his life on the waterfront was over. He spent the remainder of his life in a routine of taking long walks through San Francisco, commenting on architecture, visiting libraries, reading and writing for several hours a day, and giving occasional lectures at Berkeley.

The journalist who wants to understand mass movements, the kinds of people who belong to them, the psychological need of certain people to join them, the nature of "men of words," and the essence of propaganda will want to read *The True Believer.* And it is the kind of book that can be read over and over, with new benefits and insights discovered with each reading. Students who want a short course in collective behavior or the psychology of mass movements can read this short book and avoid the hefty academic tomes by sociologists and social psychologists.

Journalists, especially, need to understand various social movements. Hoffer explains characteristics common to all mass movements, such as their proclivity to breed fanaticism, fervent hope, enthusiasm, hatred, and intolerance. True believers, or members of mass movements, are united by a dedication, a pursuit of power, a faith, a common goal, and a spirit of self-sacrifice. Hoffer doesn't say so in so many words, but publications or other media supporting a mass movement would be staffed by true believers having these same characteristics.

A mass movement should not be confused with a civic or political organization. The latter offer a chance for self-advancement and appeal to self-interest. Not so with the mass movement, which appeals to those who don't seek self-advancement but rather desire to lose what Hoffer calls "the unwanted self." True believers, who populate mass movements, according to Hoffer, have a "faith in a holy cause," and this is simply a substitute for a lack of faith in themselves.

Hoffer's true believer is one who finds no excellence in his or her self and is ready to invest all excellence in some holy cause. When a person's own business is worth minding, says Hoffer, he or she will mind it; when it is not, the person turns to minding the business of others. The true believer's firm belief in some kind of "holy duty" toward others is "often a way of attaching our drowning selves to a passing raft." A great attraction of a mass movement is that it presents a substitute for individual hope. If our own personal interests and future seem not worth living for, we are ripe for the attractions of a mass movement. "All forms of dedication, devotion, loyalty and self-surrender," says Hoffer, "are in essence a desperate clinging to something which might give worth and meaning to our futile, spoiled lives."

The journalist might see one of Hoffer's aphorisms as particularly appropriate: "The game of history is usually played by the best and the worst over the heads of the majority in the middle." Is that not the game that journalism plays? ignoring largely the normal, everyday, typical people who are not great successes or great social villains? Do not journalists overemphasize what Hoffer calls the "failures, misfits, outcasts, criminals, and all those who have lost their footing"?

If journalists want to locate the disaffected, those likely to be fanatical members of a movement, says Hoffer, they will look to these types: the poor, misfits, malcontents, outcasts, minorities, adolescent youth, those with some vice or obsession, the impotent (in body and mind), the jobless, the inordinately selfish, and the bored.

Instrumental in stimulating and perpetuating a mass movement is what Hoffer calls a man of words, an intellectual who imperceptibly undermines established institutions and discredits those in power. This word merchant (writer, priest, artist, professor, journalist) weakens basic beliefs and loyalties and prepares the ground for the incipient mass movement. Men of words, says Hoffer, have a vanity and craving for a status above the common person. And, says Hoffer, there is an "irremediable insecurity at the core of every intellectual" that prompts his or her constant stance of fault finding.

Men of words value the search for truth, delight in the give-and-take of controversy; their dedication is primarily to argumentation and ideas, not to action and social implementation. This is left to the fanatics and faith-hungry masses, who invest the ideas of the men of words with "the certitude of the holy writ." Men of words, according to Hoffer, prepare the way for the mass movement by discrediting prevailing values and institutions, making the people ready for something new, giving slogans and a doctrine for a new faith, and undermining the convictions of the "better people"—those who can get along without a new faith.

The word is powerful, says Hoffer, and we need to fear the word as much as we fear the sword. This brings Hoffer to a discussion of propaganda, the skillful use of which has led to many startling successes of mass movements. However, Hoffer points out, propaganda cannot on its own force its way into unwilling minds. Nor can it inculcate anything completely new or keep people persuaded once they have stopped believing. It penetrates, says Hoffer, "only into minds already open, and rather than instill opinion it articulates and justifies opinions already present in the minds of the recipients."

Hoffer puts it neatly: "The gifted propagandist brings to a boil ideas and passions already simmering in the minds of his hearers. He echoes their innermost feelings." It is the frustrated who succumb mainly to propaganda. The propagandist's impassioned words trigger in the frustrated the "music in their own souls." Hoffer says that although words are necessary for preparing for a mass movement, once the movement is realized, words are no longer decisive. And he quotes Joseph Goebbels, the Nazi propaganda chief, as saying that "a sharp sword must always stand behind propaganda if it is to be really effective." So Hoffer points out that force, power, and coercion must be used in concert with propaganda for it to be truly effective.

Because a news medium, for example a newspaper, is an originator as well as a conveyer of propaganda, the editorial writer might take to heart this bit of Hofferian wisdom about propaganda: "Propaganda . . . serves more to justify ourselves than to convince others; and the more reason we have to feel guilty, the more fervent our propaganda."

Eric Hoffer provides some practical foundational insights for journalists. He gives them a clear view of true believers and their relationship to mass movements. He plumbs the depths of human nature and looks clearly at the workings of social groups. Certainly he provides insights into the powerful yearnings of the frustrated, weak-willed masses of the world, and like Erich Fromm, shows how they want a kind of freedom—not freedom of self-realization and self-expression but freedom from the burden of autonomous existence and the necessity of making free choices.

The journalist who reads Hoffer will get a down-to-earth practical education, albeit intellectually rooted, and will gain an understanding of the psychological and political forces that pull constantly at the seams of civilization. Hoffer's message, although he is careful not to make it a polemic, is that individual self-sufficiency and personal contentment are in danger of being subsumed by some or many mass movements intent on depersonalizing human existence.

[22]

AYN RAND

Most journalists, even the hard-nosed investigative types, might find the egoistic philosophy of Ayn Rand (1905–1982) a little hard to take seriously. However, this Russian emigrant turned American novelist and non-academic philosopher strikes a responsive chord in vast numbers of people who prize individualism, rationalism, and self-enhancement.

Rand is largely shunned by "professional" philosophers but nevertheless produced a large and influential body of novels and philosophical books that wielded great influence on many generations of college students in this country. Her emphasis always was on the importance of self-esteem, rational self-interest, achievement, freedom, honesty, and integrity. If these seem to overlap with values of existentialism, it should be quickly noted that Rand was far from an existentialist, mainly in her devotion to reason and scorn for emotionally motivated action.

Her novels, such as *The Fountainhead* and *Atlas Shrugged,* and her non-fictional philosophical books, such as *The Virtue of Selfishness* (1965) and *For the New Intellectual* (1961), bring into focus her philosophy of objectivism and her morality of rational self-interest. What is important for the journalist is Rand's emphasis on rationality as the core of journalism, on freedom of expression, on the possibility of objectivity, on egocentric motivation, and on meritocracy (rewarding excellence). Rand pulled no punches in her writing and was often in opposition to establishment philosophers whom she saw as basically promoting collectivism or statism in political philosophy; subjectivism in epistemology; and relativism, emotionalism, permissivism, and mysticism in aesthetics and ethics.

She saw modern culture as enthroning what to her were

invidious values: pessimism, hatred of the excellent, suspicion of the hero and of success; tolerance of mediocrity, sloth, and criminality; cynicism, permissiveness, and egalitarianism; and all forms of collectivism in which the individual sacrifices self. She often wrote and spoke of the general social hatred of the good and excellent simply for their being good and excellent.

Rand warned constantly of the prevailing hatred of values in modern America, and she declared that the term best describing 20th-century culture and defining the modern soul is nihilism. For her this term meant the hatred of values and reason, and she saw modern society striking out at the hated object and the rational position with the determination to destroy them.

In expressing her objectivist philosophy, Rand placed special stress on reason. Her "new intellectual" is someone who is directed by intellect, not a zombie guided by feelings, instincts, wishes, whims, or revelations. Such a person she called "integrated"—a thinker who is a person of action. Like the existentialist, Rand saw a strong connection between reason and freedom, saying that reason requires freedom, self-esteem, and self-confidence. And, for her, intellectual freedom cannot exist without political freedom, and political freedom cannot exist without economic freedom. So Rand would see press freedom and its corollary, intellectual freedom, tied securely to both economic and political freedom.

Does the journalist want to be virtuous? If so, says Rand, the journalist must be rational, for rationality is the fountain of all virtues. Reason is thus the only source of knowledge that serves as a guide to values and action. Although in general Rand scorned the philosophy of Kant, she does show an affinity with him when she insists that the social basis of her objectivist ethics is that life is an end in itself. For her as for Kant, every human being is an end, not a means to the ends or the welfare of others.

Religious moralists have said that if God did not exist, there would be no need for ethics because everything would be permissible. Secular ethicists have modified this to say that if society did not exist, morality would be unnecessary because any action would be as valid as another. Neither group is correct, says Rand. Ethics is a practical, self-enhancing, selfish necessity. For Rand, the fact that we live in a society does not hide the personal, self-centered need for an ethical code. Self-esteem requires it, our happiness demands it, and our life would wither without it.

So in Rand's philosophy, self-interest motivates the need for morality. It is not the person who sacrifices or forsakes life who is moral, but rather the person who creates and makes life possible. For Rand, the human life is the moral standard; a person exists for his or her own sake and does not sacrifice self to others nor others to self. A happy life is the standard and purpose of morality.

What are the basic foundation stones of Randian ethics? Here are a few: (1) rationality (a commitment to perceive reality to the best of our ability), (2) independence (a reliance on our own judgment and acceptance of responsibility for our actions), (3) honesty (never seeking values by faking reality), (4) justice (identifying people for what they are and treating them accordingly; rewarding pro-life actions and condemning anti-life actions), (5) integrity (acting according to the judgment of our consciousness), (6) productiveness (bringing knowledge, goods, or services into existence), and (7) pride (a virtue; dedication to achieving our highest potential in our character and life with no self-sacrificial tendencies).

Rand, even before finishing college in Russia, was enthralled with the philosophy of Aristotle and also became acquainted with the ideas of Friedrich Nietzsche. Her debt to Aristotle was great, especially in her development of a metaphysics of objective reality and the enthroning of individual worth. Her fascination with Nietzsche was largely fueled by the German philosopher's view of the heroic in the person and his firm opposition to collectivism and altruism.

As was true of Nietzsche, Rand's chief villain was Immanuel Kant; she saw his "duty" ethics enthroning selflessness and devaluing personal goals as moral benefits. What was ethical to

Kant was acting from duty and from duty only; action for any other reason was devoid of ethical value. Rand could not accept such a formalistic, inflexible, impersonal ethics, which she saw as leading to self-sacrifice.

Because of the influence of religion, according to Rand, the influence of sacrifice and altruism has always dominated ethics, and only a few Western thinkers have rejected this proclivity to advance "the group" at the expense of personal growth and happiness. Among them were Aristotle and Spinoza, both of whom valued the person qua person, rationality, and self-enhancement. Rand's ideas resemble such notable exceptions, but she even goes farther in opposing self-sacrifice and the cult of communitarian promoters with their goal of social stability and egalitarianism.

Freedom is another important value for Rand. Freedom of the individual vis-à-vis the state, freedom of the person threatened by institutionalized slavery, and freedom from any kind of intellectual conformity. She would have advocated maximum journalistic freedom within media institutions as well as media freedom from governmental control.

Rand would find the current journalistic emphasis on such concepts as the "people's right to know" and "the public's right of access" to the media irrational and contradictory to First Amendment provisions for a free press. Such press freedom, and even the concept of a privately owned press, would be endangered by such group-oriented rights. The first concept would force the press to divulge (publish) certain things whether it wanted to or not, and the second would take editorial decision making out of the hands of the editor or publisher and put it in the hands of some non-journalistic authority. In both instances, the traditional freedom of the press would be violated. For Rand the media owners must decide (1) what will be revealed in their media and what will not, and (2) whether or not to let certain people or groups have access to their columns. Such "public rights" would obviate editorial determination (freedom) by the media people themselves.

Epistemologically, Rand would stress the reality of objectivity for the journalist. There is, according to Rand, an objective world. All is not simply a matter of personal perception, the world being only what each person sees it to be, a subjective world that leads to a relativism in which each view of an event is as good and valid as another. Although journalists may not capture all of an objective event, objective parts can be found. And some journalists can plumb the core of reality much better than others.

Truth is truth, regardless of various versions of it expressed in journalism. Behind these bits and pieces of the truth and interpretations of the truth lies the *actual truth.* There is a truth, whether the journalist finds it or not. There is the objective reality of an event or situation; it is there, says Rand; it exists in all its objectivity regardless of its being found and revealed by human perception. The journalist should attempt to find it and understand it, not being content to despair and wallow in the sloughs of skepticism or bogs of relativism.

Rand's philosophy has much to offer the journalist, regardless of the doubts other philosophers have had about it. It provides a view based on reason, on self-esteem and pride in accomplishments, on every life-affirming activity. The Randian philosophy constantly prompts the journalist to excel, press on, be authentic, prize excellence, hate sham and hypocrisy, enthrone reason, shun conformity, love freedom, and accept personal responsibility. It is a philosophy of rational self-interest, and the idea of "rational" keeps the self-interest from deteriorating into a harmful egocentrism that wipes out all social consciousness.

The journalist who is guided by reason, not emotion or custom, will at least appreciate much of Ayn Rand's philosophy. No self-sacrificing for this journalist, for he or she will sense the ancient Aristotelian truth, emphasized by Rand more than any other in recent times, that when the individual perfects and advances self, all society is thereby strengthened.

[23]

DIETRICH BONHOEFFER

The outstanding German thinker and Lutheran theologian, Dietrich Bonhoeffer (1906–1945), had much to say of use to journalists. In many ways he reflected views expressed by Kierkegaard, especially as they related to personal existential commitment. Bonhoeffer not only opposed Hitler but was hanged by the Nazis in the spring of 1945 at the age of 39 for his involvement in attempts on Hitler's life. His whole life was a testament to courage, faith, commitment, and action.

Much of Bonhoeffer's ethical thinking can be found in *Ethics,* edited by Eberhard Bethge and published in 1955 by Macmillan Publishing Co. His ethics may be said to combine elements of *situation ethics,* which considers the specific context in ethical choice and says (see Joseph Fletcher's *Situation Ethics*) that the ethical decision stems from *agape* or Christian love, and *existential ethics,* which stresses a person's free choice and committed action.

So Bonhoeffer would merge Kierkegaard's existentialism with the American Joseph Fletcher's love-situationism into a meaningful ethics for the journalist. He would not, however, condone using situationism as a way to avoid principled action; rather, he saw it as a means to making principled decisions during situations of extreme gravity (such as the Nazi period). As for existentialism, Bonhoeffer used his free will to want Hitler's death, admitting that such a commitment was sinful but believing that it was necessary and being ready to accept personal responsibility.

Bonhoeffer would have little patience with "gutter journalists" who practice exposé journalism, invading privacy and giving the public intimate details of the lives of prominent people.

He would advocate a journalism that provides the audience thoughtful and helpful information designed to create a society of concerned citizens gravitating toward peaceful resolution of friction. Journalism that aims at what might be called the "greatest titillation principle" was not the kind of teleological ethics Bonhoeffer would advocate. Use your freedom for good, he would advise the journalist; do what you think God would approve of, and be willing to take personal responsibility for it.

Even though Bonhoeffer always considered himself a pacifist, he was a militant against Nazi racism. He accepted guilt for being a conspirator, but he believed that his actions were right at the time and in the context. A journalist, likewise, might do certain things against his or her basic nature if a higher ethical plane might be reached. Often, as Bonhoeffer stressed, it is not doing what is "right" or "wrong" but what is "best" or "better."

The journalist is concerned with freedom and responsibility. So is Bonhoeffer, and he sees such concepts as closely related—responsibility presupposing freedom and freedom consisting only in responsibility. In his *Ethics* he writes that responsibility "is the freedom of men . . . given only in the obligation to God and to our neighbour" and that the "proof of his freedom is that nothing can answer for him . . . except his own deed and his own self." The journalist might, with good reason, take these words seriously.

Many difficult choices face the journalist, and Bonhoeffer stresses that a person must face them and, hitting an existentialist note, not try to escape them or put them on others. If we, acting in a journalistic situation, must make hard decisions, Bonhoeffer says that we will not be simply deciding "between right and wrong and between good and evil, but between right and right and between wrong and wrong." So the journalist should realize that he or she may select an option that is better than another but still be doing something that is wrong.

What would Bonhoeffer think of Kant's "duty" ethics and categorical imperative? He would likely see Kant's ethics as that of a robot, a person who is programmed, set in motion, and reacts to already-determined stimuli (principles). This, for

Bonhoeffer, would obviate free determination of ethical actions by the choosing person. The journalist, for example, would have a priori principles on which to act, thereby freeing himself or herself from self-determination in specific contexts.

Clearly, however, Bonhoeffer believed in principles that should not be compromised. One such principle for the journalist might be something like this: Do only those things that, out of love and a sense of commitment to God's guidance, you feel are better than other things. This puts the ethical ball back in the journalist's court and insists on a kind of love-directed situationism in which to use existential commitment. It does not, as a priori Kantian maxims would dictate, ordain a certain action in every situation.

However, Bonhoeffer's ideas on following a priori rules at times seem a little puzzling. For instance, in his ethics he views the greatest good to be finding and following the will of God. Therefore, he would advocate following God's principles when confronted with an ethical situation. This would be in line with Kantianism. So it would appear that he is not really against deontological ("duty") ethical guidance; he is simply in favor of it coming *from God.*

One can even apply this to utilitarian (teleological) ethics. Bonhoeffer would agree with the utilitarians that what is necessary is the bringing of the greatest happiness (or good) to the greatest number. But for him, the greatest good is being in tune with God's will. Therefore, what is ethical again would be finding God's will, acting in accord with it, and spreading it to the greatest number possible. So Bonhoeffer's ethics can be reconciled with utilitarianism. Interestingly, Bonhoeffer's ethics might also be reconciled with Kantianism, in that one way Kant's duty-bound guidelines might be obtained would be to get them from God.

Bonhoeffer's concern for the downtrodden and weak in society has some affinity with John Rawls (discussed below) whose "veil of ignorance" is designed to give equality to the weaker parties in an ethical situation. Bonhoeffer would urge journalists to give more attention to the poor, weak, ill, and disadvantaged in society. More attention, Bonhoeffer would say, should be given to reporting the "humanistic concerns" of society and less to the activities of the powerful elite of government and industry.

Bonhoeffer would endorse the so-called theory of social responsibility recommended by the Commission on Freedom of the Press in 1947. His ideas coincide well with the recommendations of Hutchins' group. Especially appealing to the German theologian would have been the idea that the press is free so that it can justify itself as a servant of society, and can have a socially beneficial effect. Another link to the Commission was Bonhoffer's friendship and affinity with one of its members—theologian Reinhold Niebuhr. Bonhoeffer's main thrust in ethics was certainly one of community, social concern, societal action, and altruism prompted by *agape.* At the same time he stressed the importance of individual self-development precipitated by seeking the will of God and by personal commitment to self-improvement.

The journalist can benefit from Bonhoeffer in many ways, perhaps the most important being the example of dedication and courage that he set by his own life and death. Also extremely important was his deep concern for ethics. He had five main objectives in the area of ethics, and they have been explicated well by Dr. Herbert Strentz of Drake University in a long paper (1993) on the German theologian: (1) to stimulate the moral imagination, (2) to recognize ethical issues, (3) to elicit a sense of moral obligation, (4) to develop analytical skills, and (5) to tolerate, and reduce, disagreement and ambiguity.

All five of these objectives are essential, it would seem, to the journalist who aspires to be both moral and professionally proficient. Bonhoeffer's entire thought should encourage journalists to commitment, action, and the acceptance of personal responsibility. Such a tendency toward existentialism is moderated to a considerable degree by Bonhoeffer's sympathy with "principled action" determined by finding and following the will of God. His ability to combine a deep concern for society and the integrity of the individual person should be an example for the journalist of today.

[24]

SIMONE DE BEAUVOIR

Reflecting well the existentialist stance taken to various degrees by many of the great thinkers profiled in this book is Simone de Beauvoir (1908–1986), a French philosopher, novelist, editor, essayist, and political activist. She was influenced in her youth by such French authors as André Gide, Jean Cocteau, Paul Claudel, and Paul Valéry. While a student at the Sorbonne in 1929, she met Jean-Paul Sartre and found in him the kind of person with whom she wanted to share her life. And she did just that, living with him for 51 years, although they never married.

Much of Beauvoir's early writing had to do with personal crises and observations on various personalities with whom she came in contact. With World War II her attention shifted to more philosophical, ethical, and political issues. She, along with Sartre, tried to explain existentialism and also delved into questions of freedom, responsibility, and the importance of communication. In an essay, *Pyrrhus et Cineas,* Beauvoir dealt especially with those issues in the light of existentialist ideas that Sartre had been developing. This essay is often seen as one of the clearest presentations—a kind of popularization—of existentialist thought.

Briefly, Beauvoir said that existentialism considered a person neither naturally good nor naturally bad, emphasizing rather that one is the sole master of one's own destiny. A person, she wrote, is nothing at first, and it is up to that person to make himself or herself good or bad by using freedom or by denying it. Sin, to her, was the prevention of (from external or internal sources) free and responsible self-development. Beauvoir insisted that existentialist philosophy, because it stressed the potential of constructing one's own essence, was basically positive and optimistic.

Just how did Beauvoir view ethics? She stressed that our mortality, and the constant knowledge of our finitude, provides value to our ethical strivings—our search for good and right actions. If we lived forever, she opined, there would be no urgency or intensity, no real creation of a significant life pattern. Life, for Beauvoir, has meaning when a person finds something worth dying for; in a sense, Beauvoir believed that it is death, or the knowledge of its inevitability, that leads to ethical responsibility.

Like Sartre, she believed that there is no a priori good; we must all create good as we develop ourselves, our essences. When we choose the good, we are in effect choosing for everyone. It is necessary to take responsibility for our actions, and our actions make us who we are. One is not determined by circumstances, by environment, by events, or by others; one is determined ultimately by oneself. Only by accepting this reality can a person obtain dignity and adequately combat being reduced to an object. Beauvoir believed that there are no a priori ethical values, that they are developed during the process of living and making decisions. An ethical choice, as is true with a piece of art, can be judged only after it has been made. As we choose our ethics, we make ourselves; this is the very nature of existentialism.

Although Beauvoir's (and other existentialists') concept of the authentic free person kept her from proposing a code of ethics, she would venture a guiding principle for moral decision making. Such a principle is infused with the existentialist view that every person's life is part of the total fabric of humanity. This imposes a great responsibility on a person: When a person chooses, he or she is choosing for everyone. So we might express the existentialist Golden Rule something like this: One should choose what one would wish all other people to choose under the same circumstances.

Reminiscent of Kant's categorical imperative, this universalizing choice does not necessarily imply altruism. The existentialist, like Nietzsche, might hold that humankind should actively participate in life's struggle to be strong, thereby participating in a kind of Social Darwinism whereby the strong survive and the species is improved. And it could be, in individual cases, that a person would agree with Nietzsche that altruism is a fraud, pushed on humanity by the weak through sentimentality and religion. Another problem with the existentialist Golden Rule above is that a person, by adopting this rule, actually limits freedom of choice and slides into a mold created by other people; when this happens that person becomes less authentic.

So we can see that Beauvoir has a difficult time discussing ethics. And this is true of all existentialists because of the very personal, *self*-deterministic nature of existentialism. The moral imperatives of Immanuel Kant cannot be embraced by Beauvoir because she sees them as denying the individuality of each situation. And generally, the subject of ethics carries a *social*-deterministic emphasis. We often assume that an ethics is formulated and enforced by some group of peers or by society at large. For example, we speak of legal ethics, or medical ethics, or social ethics. And those in journalism speak of journalistic ethics. This concept of ethics binds the journalist to the norms of the group and leads him or her into a kind of conformist posture. This, of course, is repugnant to the existentialist, who has a deep-rooted allegiance to personal autonomy and individual freedom.

For Beauvoir, the Kantian universal ethics must be opposed, because the absolute, universal person does not exist. Freedom, the foundation of human existence, rebels naturally against any cold a priori Kantian formalism. But for Beauvoir, freedom must be positive (or active); it must not be simply contingent (arbitrary, directionless) action, which is negative. Passivism, quietism, or stoicism is not enough for the existentialist. Truly free actions must be meaningful and coherent, not accidental and random. The very worst for Beauvoir would be the journalist who engages in a useless repetition of tasks devoid of real enjoyment. This would render existence itself meaningless. In short, what Beauvoir says is this: ethical action, should, to the maximum extent possible, have as its end the freedom of the greatest number of human beings. Therefore, she seems to apply a kind of utilitarian calculus to a general ethical stance.

A dominant concern and emphasis of Beauvoir in much of her writing, especially during the 1960s, was women and their problems—their subservient social position, their lack of self-esteem, and their general absence from the business and political worlds. Many women saw her, and see her today, as the person who led the way in the women's movement, as a pioneer in suggesting the possibility that women could break out of the mold society had made for them. The American feminist Betty Friedan has called Beauvoir "an authentic heroine" in the history of the women's movement. Beauvoir's *The Second Sex* (1949), called by writer Philip Wylie "one of the few great books of our era," became the book around which women rallied in their campaign for liberation.

Beauvoir would relate existentialism to journalism by saying that journalists should be free and authentic and not simply cogs in the impersonal wheel of the media establishment; that they are not expendable or replaceable; that they are unique in existence and personality; that they must develop their integrity and individual personalities and project themselves into society through their actions; that they rebel against being lost, anonymous functionaries; and that they extol freedom and exercise responsibility in a day when increasing numbers of people are trying to escape freedom and blame others for the negative consequences of their actions.

Beauvoir sees responsibility as freedom's anchor; a person is responsible for each act and for the consequences of each act. Nobody else can take responsibility for what a person is; that person and that person alone must bear the responsibility. Freedom brings this heavy load of responsibility; Sartre said that a person is "condemned" to be free, and Kierkegaard wrote of the need to choose "in fear and trembling." But choose we must, for ourselves and for all others, with no assurance that our choice will be the "right" one.

Every journalist is seen by the existentialist as one who has the freedom to *try* to accomplish desired ends. For Beauvoir, the journalist who does not *will* to be free (even though he or she may fail in an endeavor) is choosing the inauthentic life. A person must take control of the mechanisms of life, must make decisions and take actions; failing this, according to Beauvoir, a person will become degraded into no more than a machine operating as a robotized instrument of someone else. Or, perhaps even worse, such a person becomes a passive object, less than human, transformed into nothing more than a stone.

Beauvoir would also tell journalists to develop an individual communication style. When journalists cherish their uniqueness, they will also cherish, develop, and protect personal journalistic style, most obvious in writing and, in the case of broadcast journalism, speaking. Style is personal—the highly individualized dimension in journalism—and is the revelation of one's self. One is tempted in corporate journalism to hide one's style, to cover it under a blanket of anonymity and conformity. But, the existentialist would insist, style is important, and the journalist who loses it, or never really develops it, commits journalistic suicide.

Style is honesty, and honesty is most important to existential authenticity and individuality. If a journalist's style is to reflect the *real* journalist, it must be honest, meaning that it must spring from an unpolluted and pure self. For style gives journalism power, variety, and charm. It is a kind of verbal magic. If the journalist is authentic, this style will manifest itself in language that makes a word sparkle, a sentence unforgettable, a passage stimulating, an article impelling and meaningful. Beauvoir tried to write, and live, with style. She, like most journalists, fell short on many occasions, but the point is that she recognized the importance of style, and she tried to develop and use this very personal dimension of the writer's craft.

Beauvoir would encourage the journalist to see fresh vistas, hear different voices, employ new techniques, and contemplate unfamiliar thoughts. The idea is to use freedom wisely to create a worthwhile self worthy of using such freedom. Journalists should always try to experiment, to push ideas into new areas, to live ever-new psychological and linguistic lives in which fresh intellectual winds batter the old frameworks of their existence. This is a worthy journalistic heritage—one that comes from a valiant, passionate, and activist representative of a long line of existentialist thinkers.

[25]

MARSHALL McLUHAN

Optimism, related largely to an expanding technology, got its most forceful exposure in the works of Marshall McLuhan (1911–1980), an exuberant Canadian professor of English literature. McLuhan, even in his heyday during the 1960s, was not treated kindly by his critics and fellow professors. Many saw his ideas as flawed, his methodologies as weak, and his thought-provoking "probes" as far-out or even ridiculous. Nevertheless, this Canadian thinker who was seriously concerned about communication made a significant impact on journalistic and communication studies, and his name still reverberates in the academic community and among television aficionados.

His optimistic theme: The mass media, especially television and radio, have the potential to bring about a better world and forge it into what he called "the global village." McLuhan published his popular *Understanding Media: The Extensions of Man* in 1964, in which he threw out his catalytic probe, "the medium is the message." He wrote that it is the medium that shapes and controls human association and action, not the content, which typically "blinds us to the character of the medium."

The manner of communicating information was, to McLuhan, most important. He was in the early wave of scholars who were to study structural aspects of communication, leading to the end-of-the-century fascination with such areas as semiotics, structuralism, structural anthropology, and linguistics. Technology, the *form* of communication—and McLuhan was thinking of radio and television—had freed people from what he called the linear world of the print media that had begun with Gutenberg.

Henceforth, he said, the previously crude and fragmented vision forced on audiences by the printed word will be broadened to be more "tribal and collective" in nature. The world is, in a sense, being remade through electronic communication into the global village, where people confront face-to-face their "chiefs" and others in their communities, freed at last from the anonymity of the printed page.

With the rise of television, McLuhan also saw a return to communal society and a decline of 18th-century individualism, which he saw as ushered in by the discovery of movable type, about which he wrote in *The Gutenberg Galaxy* in 1962. Whereas McLuhan saw the new technology of television as positive and beneficial, his fellow Canadian and teacher Harold A. Innis, another technological social determinist, conceived of it as debilitating and negative. Innis (and McLuhan had agreed with him much earlier) saw the new media as basically harmful to human beings, lowering their sensibilities, trivializing serious matters, and serving as conveyers of political and commercial propaganda.

Innis, like McLuhan, thought of technologies as shaping societies throughout history; but to him and to a majority of social and media critics before and after him, the net effect of these new communications forms was disruptive, dehumanizing, and generally unsettling. Innis, like Jacques Ellul in France (discussed below), had envisioned technological progress as exacting a high price. Why? Such technology (Ellul called it technique) makes no distinction between moral and immoral use, is unconcerned with the future, and blindly seeks its own ends and establishes its own independent technical morality. Innis' best treatises on communication and its technologies are *Empire and Communications* (1950) and *The Bias of Communication* (1951).

McLuhan was not a modest man. He won a strong following and much public attention by presuming to understand all the mysterious secrets of media (especially television) and being willing to invest such knowledge with psychological and environmental ramifications. He also predicted links between television computers, radio, and other automated devices, becoming the foremost prophet of the new "electronics" age.

Even his writing evidences a break with the older, "linear," print-oriented world. In his *Understanding Media,* for example, he presents history in a jumbled form—a kind of disjointed picture—which he calls a "mosaic" that the reader presumably must "take in" all at once. Television journalists, of course, can find much solace and hope in McLuhan's writings because they are pioneers in this new world. Newspaper and other print journalists, however, may feel some sadness because McLuhan sees their world disappearing. For McLuhan, the TV world is unifying people, bringing them together in his global village, and causing them to experience an immediately synthesized culture impossible for people of the older print-oriented communication mode.

However, in a very real sense McLuhan, in stressing the idea of the medium as the message, cut the foundation out from under all journalism. At least for the journalist interested in the content, style, substance, and effect of his or her writing, McLuhan is no inspiration. For McLuhan contends that in any form of communication or artistic message, what is consciously *said* is of no importance. Nor is the style, the way it is said, important. The only thing of importance is the medium used to say it.

Television audiences, for instance, are not affected by what they see but rather by the mere process of watching. And this, says McLuhan, is true with every medium that has appeared throughout history. What is important is that a medium plays upon the feelings, sensitivities, emotions, and intuitions of the audience members. Explicit logic, substance, and organization of the message itself means nothing; only the technological way things are communicated is important—and it is this medium and not the content that is the message.

McLuhan provided other new terms for communicators to contend with. For instance, he introduced the concepts of "hot" and "cool" media. Hot media are filled with data, whereas cool media have very few data. By data he seems to mean the effect of the medium on the senses—a very specialized meaning of the term. Media are hot if they provide "high definition" and cool if they provide "low definition." A low-definition (or cool) medium demands greater participation by the audience, requires more "filling in" by the audience. On the other hand, hot or high-definition media are low in participation, with less effort needed by the audience to experience the message.

For McLuhan, television is the coolest of the media, requiring the most audience involvement. The image on TV necessitates that an audience member constantly take part in a kind of sensuous participation that McLuhan called "profoundly kinetic and tactile." If this concept seems vague or even ridiculous, McLuhan would say it is simply because we are still stuck in the Gutenberg world of linear communication. And what is an example of a hot medium? A painting or a photograph, according to McLuhan. Looking at it requires no filling in by the audience. Printed newspapers and books are also hot or non-participatory media.

Another term that McLuhan tossed out was "retribalization." As we plunge into the global village brought on mainly by television, we are actually becoming again members of a tribe. As we neglect the media of literacy, the print media, and involve ourselves more intensely in the world of television, we in a real sense re-enter the tribe. In this new electronic world we are once again in a tactile environment, visually integrated, where we can see and hear our communitarian colleagues and come face-to-face with our chiefs.

Although McLuhan in his works zigzags through almost every historical moment and sends his impressionistic probes out in all directions, he mainly focuses on the modern electronic media. His thesis: New media establish new environments and change human senses. And new senses bring about changed people, and changed people bring about significant historical explosions. And such a process goes on over and over.

The 1960s, with their vibrant, challenging, and flashy experimentation, was the perfect era for McLuhan to soar into the academic (and pop culture) scene. But his heyday is over. His disjointed history and catalytic probes do not find much favor with today's audiences. However, his name is still heard, and his main ideas are still around. Technological optimists find him companionable. Journalists, usually more down-to-earth and skeptical of mystical exuberances, must find him rather tedious and unpalatable. McLuhan's ideas mainly deny journalists their creativity and place it in the media themselves. The media are the messages, in McLuhan's world, and journalists need not worry about such unimportant things. In a sense, they are reduced to non-creative functionaries oiling the cogs of the media structures. Not a promising and fulfilling prospect for sensitive and creative souls.

[26]

JACQUES ELLUL

Journalists don't like to think of themselves as propagandists, or censors, or information manipulators, or news managers. This is perhaps natural, but believing that they aren't is a big illusion, says Jacques Ellul (1912–), for many years a popular sociology professor at France's University of Bordeaux. Propaganda, he says, is woven into the very fabric of journalism, and journalists not only constantly transmit the propaganda of others, especially government, but also originate a multitude of persuasive messages designed to manipulate thinking and action.

His influential *Propaganda,* translated and published in the United States in 1965, was a follow-up to *The Technological Society,* a book that had thrown the author into the middle of a debate between optimists and pessimists as to whether advancing technology, including electronic media, would enhance or endanger our way of life. Ellul came down on the side of the pessimists, seeing technology as generally enslaving and robotizing the world. Certainly he saw technology as complicating society and confusing individuals with a plethora of sophisticated machines and gadgets. This put him over against such optimists as Marshall McLuhan who saw nothing but societal good in every developing technology.

Propaganda, according to Ellul, is mainly used, at least by governments, to help solve technology's problems, to mitigate the social trauma of a technological society, and to try to bring the individual into a more harmonious relationship with a world increasingly filled with machines. The mass media, says Ellul, whether creating or transmitting propaganda, make it possible for directive and persuasive messages to reach gigantic audiences simultaneously. Although Ellul deals mainly with what he calls "public" or "government" propaganda, he gives considerable attention to "private" propaganda—that disseminated by advertising, editorializing, teaching, preaching, and growing groups and constituencies with some sort of mission.

What has happened, says Ellul, is that propaganda has in a real sense become a form of necessary justification for institutional and political policy. Government propaganda, he believes, has become essential in society, where the average citizen, largely devoid of power, *needs* to have the world simplified and explained.

The American government, with power being increasingly centralized in Washington D.C., finds propaganda mandatory. The electorate, Ellul affirms, must be convinced that the world is too complex for the average person to understand; so the government is ready, willing, and able to interpret problems and suggest solutions. In a way, propaganda signals the demise of a meaningful democracy; the propagandists don't have to lie in the classic sense, but they don't trust in the critical judgment of the people. They don't withhold or falsify information but overwhelm people with facts, statistics, opinions, and interpretations.

Journalists by and large cooperate with government and its propaganda. They not only convey this propaganda to the public but, even when they are opposing some government policy, they are emphasizing the government's social agenda for concern, discussion, and action. And in addition they are dispensing propaganda from many sources—institutional, industrial, educational, and religious—and in fact are originating their own propaganda through all the press' substantial channels. They not only popularize the government's agenda, but they push an agenda of their own.

Ellul says that propaganda seeks to induce opinion, belief, participation, and action with as little thought by the propagandized as possible. In other words, propaganda is a methodology used by some organized group to bring about some sort of common belief or active or passive participation within a mass audience. Perhaps most disturbing of Ellul's views is that people want, if not crave, propaganda.

So people get what they want. And propagandists get what they want. Ellul says that democratic leaders cannot follow what he calls "irrational" public opinion, because to do so the government would be forced to cave in to "opinion of the incompetents." This leads the government to psychologically submerge the population with its propaganda—a propaganda that has become an absolute component of governance.

Not to be considered a malicious activity prompted by evil motives, propaganda, for Ellul, is simply an inescapable means of governing and keeping people relatively contented. No wicked propagandist is at work trying to mislead and ensnare the innocent and unwary citizen; rather, says Ellul, the citizen craves propaganda and the propagandist responds to this need.

By the time citizens come to the media as young adults, they are ready for propaganda's more active efforts. Ironically, Ellul theorizes that as the population becomes more educated, it becomes more easily led by propaganda—especially that coming from government. Ellul says that, beginning with primary schools and going through college, educational systems fill students' minds with complex, contradictory, unsynthesized, and superficial information, which he calls "pre-propaganda." The educated class, then, is set up for government public relations, for more sophisticated, persuasive, "answer-giving" communication. The poor and illiterate have little to fear from the propagandist, according to Ellul, because they are not tuned in, and besides, they're spending their time trying to stay alive.

The newspaper reader, for instance, gets a steady diet of news that focuses on disaster and calamity, on sensation and negativism, on corruption and criminality, pointing out the danger and chaos of society. This, Ellul contends, contributes to the readers' interpretation of the world as absurd, incoherent, and irrational. The basic nature of the news, as well as its volume, confuses audience members and makes them ready for the simple answers of the propagandist.

Propaganda's basic nature reduces and simplifies all issues. It plants in people a basic two-valued orientation—black/white, good/bad, right/wrong, conservative/liberal. The journalist, who should want to present a representative, multidimensional picture of reality, contributes to this black-and-white picture through simplistic and often propagandistic stories. And by and large their audiences are ready to accept such stories. No need to think, compare, and question; simply accept the solutions and explanations provided by the propagandist. And even when many people think they are repelling propaganda, they are being affected—in subtle ways perhaps, but affected nevertheless.

Government as a propagandist receives most concern from Ellul, but other propaganda institutions, such as the press, also get considerable attention. Most government propaganda reaches us via the mass media, not from government media themselves. Therefore, the journalist, at least in a democratic society, must be especially careful not to be a mere servant of the government, simply passing on the raw state propaganda to an unsuspecting, but willing, citizenry. As Ellul says, governments in all societies, but especially in capitalistic democracies, do not need to invest heavily in their own media. They have a ready-made system of conveyance in the free press of their countries.

A most interesting idea that Ellul throws out is that, in countries like the United States, the media do themselves no favor by expanding their freedom. Increased freedom simply means a demand for more propaganda sought from government by the press. In effect, the freer the press, the more it demands information (propaganda) from the government. Here Ellul is not talking about the *quality* of information received from government by the press; rather, he is referring to the total amount or *quantity* of government-inspired propaganda. Said another way: A free press allows government propaganda a wide, constant, and ever-expanding forum. In a system of authoritarian journalism, the government is forced to use primarily its own resources and media to get the word out.

Technology, says Ellul, is largely responsible for the increasing potency of propaganda. Journalists, for example, are largely slaves of their newly acquired technological innovations. Less and less do they have a personal relationship with the content itself; more and more they rely on the easy acquisition of information from data banks and other communication facilitators. The government knows this and is busy saturating the communication stream with easily accessed propaganda. Journalists, then, who want to retain maximum autonomy in the face of technology and who smart under the barrage of government propaganda awaiting transmission, must be ever more careful to negate the effect of such propaganda by more careful screening.

Not that Ellul thinks the government has evil motives or anti-people designs. It is simply a matter of journalistic integrity; if the media rebel at being "used," they will become increasingly propaganda managers, having increased power over their own propaganda and the propaganda of others. However, there is no way to eliminate propaganda, even if it were a good thing to do so. Journalists need it to function; the government needs it to sustain itself and progress; and people need it to simplify the complex reality around them and to at least *think* they understand it.

The journalist, by and large, will not be reassured by Ellul. The French scholar, for example, believes that news does not help the audience member become a better citizen or a more knowledgeable voter. On the contrary, says Ellul in his book *The Political Illusion,* news (filled as it is with attention-getting propaganda) inundates the recipient with far more information than can be absorbed, information that is too diverse to be of any real service. News basically titillates and moves on quickly to titillate again, offering no consistent and meaningful picture of any event or idea. And so journalism, says Ellul, creates a "stupefying lack of continuity," which leaves the audience member more perplexed than edified, more confused than educated, more anxious than reassured.

[27]

BARBARA TUCHMAN

Pulitzer prize-winning historian Barbara Tuchman (1912–1989) probably has more to say to today's journalist about the craft of writing than any other 20th-century American thinker. Although she was a popular historian (as contrasted to an academic one; she had only a bachelor's degree from Radcliffe), she received both popular and critical acclaim for her narrative histories and was awarded two Pulitzer prizes.

She spent some time (1933–39) in journalism, serving as a research and editorial assistant, staff writer, and foreign correspondent for *The Nation* magazine. She was sent to Spain in 1937 by the magazine to cover the Spanish Civil War. From 1943 to 1945 Tuchman was an editor for the Office of War Information in New York City. She was a lecturer at Harvard, the University of California, the U.S. Naval War College, and other universities and institutions. She received honorary doctorates from at least a dozen American universities.

Reflecting her journalistic inclinations, Tuchman stressed lean, clear writing—short, pungent sentences that tell a lucid and crisp story. What she says about writing history can easily be applied to the journalist. Her key: Eliminate wordiness, banish obscurity, select critically, have an element of suspense, and research carefully. Tuchman saw not having been trained as a historian as no great disadvantage. She noted at one point that perhaps not getting a doctorate kept her from ruining her writing style. For her stories, she relied on first-hand knowledge of the subject, meticulous research, visiting the actual sites of events, conducting many interviews, and having a writing style that keeps the reader interested.

She won a Pulitzer Prize in 1963 for *The Guns of August* (which was also a Book-of-the-Month Club selection), the story of the opening days of World War I; a *New Yorker* reviewer called it "a nearly perfect literary triumph." She won her second Pulitzer in 1971 for her book *Stilwell and the American Experience in China, 1911–1945*. Several of her other popular histories are *The Zimmermann Telegram* (1958), *The Proud Tower* (1966), *The March of Folly: From Troy to Vietnam* (1984), and a book of special importance to the journalist because of its insights into research and writing, *Practicing History: Selected Essays,* published in 1981.

One of her most "literary" histories, *A Distant Mirror* (1978), is about the 14th century, which she saw in many ways as similar to the 20th. The book was hailed by the *New York Review of Books* as "beautifully written, careful and thorough in its scholarship, extensive in the range of topics peripherally touched upon, and enlivened by consistently intelligent comment." According to Laurence Freedman, writing in the *Times Literary Supplement* (London), Tuchman is always "a pleasure for the layman to read." He noted that she brings to her writing a "flair for the dramatic, a striking ability to combine narrative sweep with individual character analysis, and a vividly entertaining prose style."

The journalist would be wise to take Tuchman's admonitions and thoughts about writing seriously. Probably the best book for this advice is *Practicing History,* a collection of Tuchman's essays. The following insights are selected from this book; the journalist or journalism student wanting some valuable guidance on writing (with Tuchman illustrating her points by her own writing style) would do well to read it.

Tuchman's concern for quality writing may best be found in the essay titled "The Historian as Artist." It could just as well be called "The Journalist as Artist." Here she champions the idea that history (read: journalism) can be "creative"—an art, if you will—just like poetry and fiction. Tuchman makes her signature point in this essay that writing should be for the general reader, not just for a few fellow scholars. Reason: When you write for the public you have to be clear and interesting—the two foundational criteria of good writing.

Many creative journalists with "literary" flair can resonate to this statement:

> I have always *felt* like an artist when I work on a book but I did not think I ought to say so until someone wise said it first. . . . Now that an occasional reviewer here and there has made the observation, I feel I can talk about it. I see no reason why the word should always be confined to writers of fiction and poetry while the rest of us are lumped together under that despicable term "Nonfiction"—as if we were some sort of remainder.

Tuchman would see historians and journalists as artists, or at least as having the potential to be artists. The artist, she says, has an *extra* vision and an *inner* vision, "plus the ability to express it." Such a writer, an artist, can supply an understanding that the reader could not have had without the aid of what Tuchman calls "the artist's creative vision."

Tuchman's examples of writers of non-fiction who were writers of literature also include Lytton Strachey, who perceived a truth about Queen Victoria and other eminent Victorians in a style and form that revolutionized the whole approach to biography; Rachel Carson, who perceived truth about the seashore and the "silent spring"; Thoreau, about Walden Pond; Tocqueville and James Bryce about America; Gibbon, about Rome; Karl Marx, about economic classes and the effect of capitalism; Carlyle, about the French Revolution. "Their work," wrote Tuchman, "is based on study, observation, and accumulation of fact, but does anyone suppose that these realists did not make use of their imagination? Certainly they did; that is what gave them their extra vision."

Journalists and historians, says Tuchman, in order to be artists must perceive a truth (historical or journalistic); then they must gather evidence and convey that truth to the reader, not by piling up a list of all the facts they have collected, "which is the way of the Ph.D.," but by "exercising the artist's privilege of selection."

According to Tuchman, there are three parts to the creative process: (1) the extra vision with which the artist sees a truth and conveys it by suggestion, (2) the medium of expression: language (for writers), paint (for painters), clay or stone (for sculptors), and musical sound (for composers), and (3) design or structure. As to language, Tuchman says that there is nothing more satisfying than to write a good sentence: "It is no fun to write lumpishly, dully, in prose the reader must plod through like wet sand." To write well, she says, requires hard work, skill, a good ear, and practice—just as much practice "as it takes Heifetz to play the violin." The writer's goals: clarity, interest, and aesthetic pleasure.

Tuchman deals with a problem facing every journalist: structure, which she says is mainly a problem of selection. Selection is "an agonizing business because there is always more material than one can use or fit into a story." Every journalist knows this problem: what to select out of all that happened without giving a certain overemphasis or underemphasis that does harm to the truth. And what is a temptation in all this? Tuchman admits that one must fight constantly against selecting what will suit one's own biases. It is a never-ending fight for the historian and journalist. Another difficult part of a story's structure is that of explaining causes and providing adequate background without letting the flow of the story bog down. "If anyone thinks this does not take creative writing," Tuchman says, "just try it."

Tuchman does not think that journalists are historians, although she does not rule out the possibility of their being artists. Journalists, she says, are on the level of "I-was-there recorders," whose accounts contain useful information "buried in a mass of daily travelogue which the passage of time has reduced to trivia." But she admits that some of the most vivid details of her histories came from the working press. The journalist, she believes, is too close to the event to get much perspective or truth into the story. There is not enough detachment, not enough distance, not enough time for interpretation and analysis. Journalism, or "contemporary history," as it is sometimes called, is extremely difficult because of the effects of "involvement." Such feelings of involvement make it even more difficult to have objectivity.

But Tuchman admits that distance does not assure objectivity, and the historian as well as the journalist must consider objectivity as a question of degree. We may be relatively objective. But this, she insists, is not the same thing as not taking sides or being neutral. "There is no such thing as a neutral or purely objective historian," she says. And no doubt she would say the same about a journalist. Historians and journalists, in her view, must have opinions: "Without an opinion a historian would be simply a ticking clock, and unreadable besides."

Tuchman would tell journalists to integrate literary devices into their journalism. She certainly said that historians should. Her education at Radcliffe was in literature and history primarily, and she learned that the two can be mutually beneficial—history illuminating literature and literature illuminating history. A sense of literature will direct non-fiction writing (history or journalism) into paths leading to more reader enjoyment and more substantive recall. Journalism or history, says Tuchman, should be written "so as to enthrall the reader and make the subject as captivating and exciting" as it is to the writer. But this is important: The writer must be enthralled and feel a drive to communicate this magic.

How does one learn to write? Tuchman's answer in her essay "In Search of History": in the practice thereof, and in having a good ear. "After seven years' apprenticeship in journalism I discovered that an essential element for good writing is a good ear. One must *listen* to the sound of one's own prose. This, I think, is one of the failings of much American writing. Too many writers do not listen to the sound of their own words."

The journalist as well as the historian should try to provide the various principal perspectives of an event. Bias in sources is to be expected. The writer allows for it and tries to correct it by providing other sources for the reader. Tuchman says: "Even if an event is not controversial, it will have been seen and remembered from different angles of view by different observers. If the event *is* in dispute, one has extra obligation to examine both sides. As the lion in Aesop said to the Man, 'There are many statues of men slaying lions, but if only the lions were sculptors there might be quite a different set of statues.' "

Nuggets of wisdom about writing non-fiction are sprinkled all through *Practicing History,* and the journalist will not have trouble digging them out. Tuchman's emphasis in this book is the craft of writing—and writing like an artist, writing in a way to be both informative and interesting and to be entertaining for the reader. This can be done with serious subjects, as Tuchman showed in her own historical writing. There is no doubt that it can be done, perhaps equally as well or better, in journalism.

The whole business of research, observation, and interviewing is hard work, although it may be "endlessly seductive," as Tuchman says. Writing is not for the faint of heart, not for the lazy, not for the pedestrian, not for the unimaginative or the plodder. At its best, it is, even in its non-fiction forms, a work of art. It is an altogether satisfying pursuit despite its laborious dimensions, and Tuchman expresses the essence and joy of writing well in these words:

> One has to sit down on that chair and think and transform thought into readable, conservative, interesting sentences that both make sense and make the reader turn the page. It is laborious, slow, often painful, sometimes agony. It means rearrangement, revision, adding, cutting, rewriting. But it brings a sense of excitement, almost of rapture; a moment on Olympus. In short, it is an act of creation.

[28]

IRIS MURDOCH

The Irish-born English novelist and philosopher Iris Murdoch (1919–) provides for the modern journalist an ethical stance based on detachment from the strong bonds of egoism and infused with a deep concern for connecting with others and a sense of altruism. In her novels (such as *The Philosopher's Pupil,* 1983) and her non-fiction books (such as the wide-ranging *Metaphysics as a Guide to Morals,* 1992) Murdoch examines the abstract ideas of moral philosophy, the meaning of good and evil, and the role of art and religion. She has much to say to the journalist, especially about the importance of characterization, the inadequacy of language to convey truth, and the ethics of moving away from self to connect with others.

Murdoch poses a counterargument to the American Ayn Rand's philosophy of rational self-interest (discussed above). She stresses that a person can come closer to virtue and "the good" by shedding the ego-ridden proclivities of the human being and moving away from the self. She shows Platonist and Christian influences in that she sees moral development as the self is sacrificed or minimized for the sake of society or others. She would also say that the writer's (read: journalist's) ethical objective is to provide a just view of reality. This is extremely difficult because of the damaging effects of egoism—seeing the world through a narrow and biased perspective.

Ranking among the top five novelists writing in England during the last half of the 20th century, Murdoch has dealt mainly with the concepts of love, freedom, and power; love is especially connected to the nature of the good. For her, the key to greater freedom is love, which she sees as cherishing the otherness of others. As she exemplifies in her fiction and non-fiction, it is this highest human achievement—love—that will save humanity.

Her novels stress the complexities of morality, the purpose of existence, and how we should live and die. Critics have compared her to Fyodor Dostoevsky, Charles Dickens, George Eliot, and Henry James. Her first book, *Sartre, Romantic Rationalist* (1953), dealt with Sartre's techniques for conveying his political views through his novels. Many began to connect Murdoch with existentialism, but she renounced that philosophy early in her career. The French writer and mystic Simone Weil's works on ethics had a great effect on Murdoch, especially on her emphasis on paying attention to others as a stimulus to ethical progress.

After World War II, Murdoch (who had studied literature and philosophy at Oxford) was offered a grant in philosophy at Cambridge, where she came under the influence of Ludwig Wittgenstein's logical positivism. In 1948 she became a fellow of St. Anne's College, Oxford, and taught philosophy. In those days and ever since she has emphasized moral philosophy and given less consideration to linguistic analysis. She has dealt in her writings with the inadequacy of language to provide a valid picture of reality. Murdoch ceased her full-time teaching in 1963 to devote greater attention to her writing.

Murdoch would tell the journalist that a firmness in trying to present the truth is a basic step on the road to morality. The journalist has a moral responsibility to provide a just vision of reality, one that encompasses the varied and complex aspects of people in the news. As she presents her linguistic philosophy of verbal inadequacy, she sounds much like Alfred Korzybski and the general semanticists. Murdoch also puts a burden of responsibility on readers, believing that they should transcend the barrier of egoism as they attempt to perceive truth. Here she is reiterating a common theme: We should be aware of, and concerned about, the damaging effects of egoism.

Another reason for communication failure is the diverse backgrounds of communicants. This audience heterogeneity is found especially in the mass audiences to which journalists have to direct their messages. What a communicator usually does, says Murdoch, is to deal in generalizations instead of addressing various and specific details and meanings. And generalizations hide any real meaning and obscure the precision needed for clear understanding. The journalist, for example, is especially guilty of giving superficial substance to characters in a story. There is no real development of the story's personalities: they are merely police, council members, lawyers, carpenters, realtors, or teachers. Murdoch's question: How can we describe a human being justly? It is a question that should plague the journalist constantly.

The journalist, according to Murdoch, will find linguistic precision and moral improvement very difficult. It is difficult for someone in a position of power, as a journalist is, to rise above personal motivations and egocentric concerns and to connect with others. It is difficult for the journalist to think of people as complex and multifaceted human beings; it is all too easy to caricature them with broad journalistic brush strokes. And it is especially difficult to realize that people exist in their own right and not simply as extensions of the journalistic self. Considering people as means and not as ends is, for Murdoch as it was for Kant, a formidable barrier to moral development.

Murdoch's moral philosophy is a mixture of Christianity and Buddhism—the mystical component is great—and she develops an argument for replacing God with the good as the focal point of a person's attention. Why? Because people who focus on things of value, like virtuous people and great art and the concept of goodness itself, have a much greater chance to improve themselves morally. She sees aesthetic appreciation as helpful in developing an ethical sensitivity; both beauty and art, for her, are moral stimulants. Individuals, in order to progress along an ethical path, must defeat the ego and merge with the transcendent good represented by humanity itself.

The journalist, trying to provide the truth, must banish egoistic motives and give the subject of the story detached, unselfish, dispassionate, and objective attention. Only then, says Murdoch, can truth (which she calls the "proper object of love") be conveyed. All false perceptions of the truth stem from ego-directed fantasy devoid of human interconnectedness.

Murdoch's Platonist philosophy manifests itself in that she believes that the truth is unreal and that individuals perceive it only as an illusion, shadow, or imperfect reflection. The same goes for the good, or moral perfection. A person, she believes, can display only that degree of truth which is in harmony with his or her spiritual development. For Murdoch, truth, aesthetics, and moral philosophy are closely related. Becoming a kind of transcendent person, detached from ego and attending to the concerns of others—this gives the individual a capacity for moral advancement. Since this is most difficult to accomplish, Murdoch sees a spiritual void in Western consciousness fueled by a growing inadequacy of human communication.

Although Murdoch disavows existentialism, many of her concepts reflect that philosophy. For example, she talks of the accidental and contingent nature of human existence, the deep feelings we have of insecurity and instability, the inability to control one's life, the constant angst associated with the knowledge of death, and the feeling that a world of fear and horror is always just around the corner. But on the positive side, Murdoch stresses individual freedom and the potential for making oneself, at least inwardly, more meaningful and potent in the battle against the uncertainties of life.

Like most existentialists, Murdoch has thrown out the traditional concept of God and does not believe in a life after death. But as mentioned above, she retains the religious or spiritual format by substituting the good for God. She believes that people should be good just for the sake of being good, that they should not need the motivation of some reward or punishment such as a heaven or hell. She deals specifically with these issues in *The Sovereignty of Good* (1971). Her religion combines features of Buddhist, Christian, and Jewish concepts, and she puts much stock in a kind of mystical, transcendental openness and awareness of the world. This awareness, and with it, moral progress, is brought about by the individual's increased consideration of other people.

In summary, Iris Murdoch provides the journalist with a blueprint for moral progress; the key to her ethics is love—a caring for and a connecting with other human beings and a retreat from egocentric motivations. The ethical person, for Murdoch, is not assertive, but humble; not self-concerned, but other-concerned; not concerned with worldly attachments, but with metaphysical or spiritual inspiration. When journalists learn to sublimate self, they begin to acquire a sense of moral awareness that pushes them onto a higher level of consciousness. And this new consciousness ushers them, through a kind of spiritual or metaphysical intuition or sense, into an enhanced moral vision. And, for Murdoch, a person's moral vision always precedes right action.

[29]

JOHN RAWLS

Journalists claim to be profoundly interested in justice; a great many of them see journalism as the means to provide social justice, to advance ideas and information that will lead to social progress and human betterment. The contemporary Harvard philosopher John Rawls (1921–), coalescing and rearranging ideas of leading thinkers of the past, has provided a concept of justice that is often cited by media ethicists as helpful to journalists.

Rawls' popular book *A Theory of Justice* (1971) provides a view of justice as *fairness,* which would be accepted by free and rational people from positions of equality in which everyone is ignorant of their place in society—class positions, social status, natural assets and abilities, intelligence, and the like. He refers to this initial position, which he compares to the state of nature in social contract theory, as being behind a "veil of ignorance."

In such a situation of equality, a journalist (for example) would determine the just thing to do by determining the fairest option. The journalist would make the ethical decision divorced from any vested interests and by dispassionately considering what is fair. Such a theoretical technique would, presumably, protect the interests of the most vulnerable or weakest of the parties involved. All people going behind this veil of ignorance would have to forget who they are, what their own values and ideologies are, and step into the shoes of the other principals of the ethical situation.

Such a situation would force journalists to set aside their own identities and make decisions by temporarily considering the viewpoints and interests of others. Many people would call this the "empathic theory" of ethics. But Rawls' idea is that the anonymous principals would have a theoretical discussion, with none of them knowing for sure what their ultimate identities will turn out to be after the veil of ignorance is lifted. The best (fairest and most just) decision would be the one that all would agree on.

At this point, we should raise a basic question: Why assume that all will reach agreement on any possible ethical solution? Even behind Rawls' veil of ignorance it is likely that the participants will choose different ethical paths. However, Rawls says that the principles of justice will be chosen behind this veil of ignorance and that no one will have an advantage over another in the choice of these principles. Because all participants are equally advantaged, according to Rawls, "the principles of justice are the result of a fair agreement or bargain and perhaps the question will be answered."

Rawls believes that justice will come forth from a discussion by rational and *equal* people concerned with their own interests but without anyone being advantaged or disadvantaged. For Rawls such discussion among equals will lead to what he calls a "reflective equilibrium" in which a consensus emerges and the group's judgments and principles conform.

Admittedly, such an original position in the real world of journalism would be difficult, and even Rawls admits that it is "purely hypothetical." It is not easy for a journalist, trying to get at the facts of a story, to provide full-disclosure reporting, to erase his or her identity and meet with sources and principals of the story in an equal and anonymous manner. This would be tantamount to stepping outside his or her professional status as a reporter. And the question immediately surfaces: Can, and should, a reporter discard journalistic identity (duties, prerogatives, status, etc.) in order to play on Rawls' so-called level playing field?

Rawls says that Kantian ethics bears a close affinity with his. The veil of ignorance is implicit in Kant's ethics. According to Rawls, the principles the Kantian acts on are not chosen because of the actor's social position or natural endowments or because of the kind of society in which the ethical dilemma occurs; for Kant, as for Rawls, what is chosen (according to the categorical imperative) is a principle of conduct applying to a person because of his or her nature "as a free and equal rational being." It should be noted that it is Rawls, not Kant, who includes and stresses the word equal.

The idea in Rawls' theory of justice of considering the concerns and interests of the weaker party or parties in ethical decision making is hardly revolutionary. His veil of ignorance does deal with the weaker party explicitly, but it should be said that *any* legitimate ethical approach necessarily takes into consideration *all* parties, including the weaker ones. This and other criticisms of Rawls' approach are given by David L. Schaefer in *Justice or Tyranny? A Critique of John Rawls's "A Theory of Justice"* (Port Washington, N.Y.: Kennikat Press, 1979).

One problem inherent in Rawlsian ethics is the impression that it degrades or devalues the person of ability, the person who achieves much in life. Rawls sees such a person as merely lucky, having been blessed at birth by a desirable social environment or superior natural attributes. Such people, Rawls would say, have no moral claims and deserve no advantages—the situation found behind the veil of ignorance. One writer who bases his main criticism on this particular point in Rawls' theory is Leonard Peikoff in his *Ominous Parallels* (New York: New American Library, 1982). He sees Rawls as concluding that nobody can "earn" values, that a person does not *deserve* any special rights because he or she does not emerge from the womb as a zero but with unearned advantages or disadvantages.

Peikoff calls this Rawlsian attitude "not merely a political but a metaphysical attack on the men of ability: it disqualifies them from moral standing." This is not a rational approach, says Peikoff; rather, it is based on sentimentality and emotionalism. Kant, he says, described his denial of reason as a defense of "pure reason," whereas Rawls—a follower of Kant—calls his own viewpoint "a theory of justice."

Another contemporary philosopher, Mortimer J. Adler, in

his *Six Great Ideas* (New York: Collier Books, 1981), sees as a serious error Rawls' identifying justice with fairness in the dealings of people with one another as well as in actions taken by a society in dealing with its members. Adler calls Rawls' *Theory of Justice* a "widely discussed and overpraised book," which casts fairness as the only principle of justice. This is not so, says Adler, who sees fairness (treating equals equally and unequals unequally in proportion to their inequality) as only one of several principles of justice, and not even the primary one.

Wrong acts, Adler points out in noting Rawls' faith in the veil of ignorance, can occur within a situation of equality or inequality. Such acts can occur even among equals behind a veil of ignorance; they are unjust because they violate a right. Bringing equality and non-equality into the equation, according to Adler, is not helpful to a discussion of justice. Such things as theft, libel, rape, and murder, Adler believes, are violations of the moral or civil law and all unjust without being in any manner unfair. They are violations of natural or legal rights; that is what their injustice consists of, and not in their being unfair.

Another critic, John Gray of Oxford University (writing in *The New York Times Book Review,* May 9, 1993), has great praise for Rawls' *Theory of Justice,* which he calls a classic that has renewed liberal thought in British and American intellectual life. But, writing specifically of Rawls' 1993 book *Political Liberalism,* he opined that Rawls departs from the earlier liberalism (and for Gray the truer version) of John Stuart Mill, with its concept of pluralism of viewpoints, and proposes a set of basic rights and liberties immune from the vagaries of political struggle.

For Gray, true liberalism should be pluralistic and must not deny that "the good" can be found in "a diversity of incommensurable conceptions." But, as Gray sees it, Rawls' 1993 book falls short in the narrowness of its perspective, the parochialism of its concerns, and its silence on major political issues. His final verdict of the book is severe: "The most striking feature of *Political Liberalism* is its utter political emptiness."

Regardless of the criticism of Rawls' specific ideas, journalists can receive from them a heavy dose of social concern and an egalitarian approach that be may of considerable value to them. Just how much a concept such as Rawls' veil of ignorance can be helpful in the daily work of the journalist is arguable, but its consideration will go far in raising journalists' social consciousness and lessening the strong pull of egocentrism.

Too much of Rawls might indeed be harmful to journalists with a dispassionate stance—still an ideal in some countries—but it might also help them to develop a greater concern and sensitivity for the social "underclasses" and to understand and appreciate the complex nature of their society and the kind of contractual agreement inherently found in it. Journalists with a bent for developing "communitarianism" that focuses on the spirit of community will see Rawls' ideas as relevant; for a moderate descendant of Marxism (and to a large extent of Christianity), such a stance would push the individual toward social consciousness and responsibility.

[30]

SISSELA BOK

Sissela Ann Bok (1934–) is a modern philosopher who has evidenced a great interest in the press and especially in the ethics of those who practice journalism. She was born in Stockholm, Sweden, and became a U.S. citizen in 1959. Bok was educated at the Sorbonne, Washington University, and Harvard, receiving her doctorate there in 1970. She has taught and lectured in philosophy at several universities and has served on many boards and committees concerned with medical ethics.

Her best-known books are *Lying: Moral Choice in Public and Private Life* (1978) and *Secrets: On the Ethics of Concealment and Revelation* (1982), both dealing significantly with the ethical problems of journalists. In *Lying,* Bok analyzes lying in many public arenas but gives much attention to the ramifications (generally negative) of journalistic lying. She does, however, differ from other philosophers (especially Kant) in believing that lying is sometimes justified. She believes that when one can avoid harm in special situations, this avoidance can override the principle of truthfulness. Other topics dealt with in *Lying* that are especially important to journalists include using silence, avoiding subjects altogether, and telling harmless ("white") lies. Often, for instance, journalists will not fabricate outright but will ignore certain aspects of a story that would add to its facticity or total truth. According to Bok, this is generally not ethical and certainly is not a sign of good professional reporting.

Bok offers relevant insights on the ethics of truth telling by incorporating a broad philosophical tradition into *Lying* and also later in *Secrets.* References to and quotations from such philosophers as Henry Sidgwich, Immanuel Kant, St. Augustine, and St. Thomas Aquinas enrich her discourse on lying and provide additional perspectives for the reader. In essence, Bok is generally in favor of a journalist telling the truth, but she does believe that lying is justified on occasion in special situations.

In Chapter 16 of *Secrets,* titled "Investigative Journalism," Bok gives attention to the reportorial problems of the journalist and especially the dialectical clash between the values of concealment and exposure, of the people's right to know and the right of privacy. Bok believes that the media and journalists have a public mandate to probe and expose secrecy in commercial and governmental circles. Journalists should be motivated and free to counterbalance the deep-seated secrecy found in public institutions. Although the press is free to try to unearth information about institutions of society (and about government, especially), it is constantly hampered by claims of confidentiality and by the natural inclination of institutions to keep secrets.

Bok poses these important questions: "Should journalists recognize limits to what they can legitimately probe and to the means for doing so? Or would such restraints inevitably threaten independent reporting and the freedom of expression?" In the chapter on investigative journalism, these questions cause her to concentrate on the fuzzy area in which a person's desire for privacy and the press's desire for public exposure conflict.

Bok, in discussing the exposure of private lives, recounts the story of William James Sidis, who had been a child prodigy but later shunned his former celebrity status. In 1937 James Thurber wrote about him in the *New Yorker* magazine, and that essay precipitated a lawsuit that went all the way to the Supreme Court.

Sidis had been exploited as a child by his psychologist father, who wanted to produce a genius. The child learned to read and write in English and French in his very early years, at 5 had written an essay on anatomy, and at 8 showed great maturity in mathematics. At 9, young Sidis went to Tufts College and two years later transferred to Harvard, where he excelled in his classes. But William Sidis found all the publicity offensive and his manipulated life unacceptable. He rejected the future his father had planned for him, stopped displaying his mental gifts, and dropped out of graduate school. He wanted his childhood kept secret; he worked at a series of menial jobs, and at age 39 he was living alone in a shabby bedroom in south Boston. It was here that James Thurber found him, giving him more unwanted publicity through the *New Yorker* story. The article was a serious blow to Sidis, putting the spotlight again on the life he wanted to hide. And, he believed, it held him up to ridicule. So he sued for invasion of privacy, claiming that the magazine held him up to public scorn, ridicule, and contempt and caused him mental anguish and humiliation.

Sidis lost the suit and an appeal. The case went to the Supreme Court, but the highest court refused to hear it. Bok seems to sympathize with Sidis but feels that if the courts had acceded to his claims, much reporting about matters of public importance could have been endangered—"every shady venture could then try to hide behind similar claims to invasion of privacy." As it happened, in 1944 this man who felt vulnerable and persecuted by the press was found unconscious in his room and died.

It would be wrong, according to Bok, for journalists to write only about people who give their consent. Reporters should be suspicious of those who use secrecy to hide abuses and resort to claims of privacy and confidentiality—or government officials who plead national security. Reporters should not accept such claims without much thought and investigation. For example, she maintains, "the serious illness of a political candidate or the paranoia of a government leader are surely matters for legitimate public concern." Health officials, she says, should not hide these matters or lie about them; nor, she insists, should journalists hide them from the public through a sense of sympathy.

One difficulty with such journalistic decisions, Bok points out, is that (as in the Sidis case) the public's interest in a story is often not based on a real *need* to know about the event. People may well have a curiosity to know, but this is not a legitimate (or ethical) reason to let them know. Bok maintains that the variation in the need to know "engenders a difference in the degree to which reporters should respect requests for anonymity and privacy." There may well be a need to know about a government official misusing public funds, but this is quite different from knowing about a private person desiring to live outside the public spotlight.

Bok puts her finger on one of the main problems: the confusing expression "the public's right to know." She says it is used to justify press coverage of almost anything—catering to both need and interest on the part of the public—regardless of the degree of legitimacy. She even quotes from the Society of Professional Journalists' Code of Ethics, which states that "the public's right to know of events of public importance and interest is the overriding mission of the mass media," and that "journalists must be free of obligations to any interest other than the public's right to know." *Any interest other than the public's right to know:* Now that is a big order! What, one might ask, about the interest of fairness? Does not the very fact of a code of ethics imply a consideration of other (ethical) reasons or interests?

Bok presents a fascinating discussion of the public's right to know, challenging many of the traditional beliefs about its validity and sanctity. She goes over the basic rationales given for such a right, especially the claim that the First Amendment presupposes such a right. If not, many say, there would be no need for the amendment. But she says that no evidence is "offered for the link; and it is not clear why, even in the absence of an underlying right to know, the freedom of speech and of the press would not be thought indispensable." Others, she says, argue that a right to speak or write implies a right to know. Bok disagrees, saying that we cannot argue from a person's right to disseminate a story to the public's right to the information it contains.

Bok then gets into a very interesting area, noting that a right to know would correspond to a duty to reveal: "the government has the duty to reveal that which the public has a right to know." Not only government, but the press itself, would have an obligation placed upon it to let the people know. But, one might ask, what about *press freedom,* which says that the press can print or not print, that it has "editorial self-determination"? Does not a free press have the right to keep people from knowing? Sadly, this is a question that Bok does not take up. But she does bring up the *obligation* aspect of a right to know, and we may wonder why, if there is such an obligation placed on government (or on the press), citizens are not furnished with free copies of newspapers and magazines as well as equipment for receiving radio and TV programs.

In her summing up of this topic, Bok points out that the public's right to know, even where partially provided by statute (such as in the Freedom of Information Act), cannot be a right to truth or to knowledge but only to access to some information. The public does have an interest in and a need for information regarding matters affecting its welfare—quite apart from the validity of any "right." And, as Bok says, if the press is to "fulfill its public mandate," it should give maximum access to this needed information. Bok does not discuss the source of this public mandate, but journalists might well wonder where they get it. Individual privacy must be considered by the press; it is in this respect, she says, that the story about William Sidis went too far. Although its publication did not violate the law, it did go beyond the bounds of moral justification.

Bok, in the "Investigative Journalism" chapter of *Secrets,* also discusses the ethically shady practice of "reporters in disguise," of misrepresentation and dishonesty in the collection of information for stories. Even if a reporter thinks such practices can be justified, Bok says that this is deceptive journalism. And, as she suggests, the argument that the press's opponents are so powerful and secretive that journalistic deception is necessary is not an ethical rationale; rather, it is a Machiavellian one. The ends justify any means, even unethical ones. Bok says such an argument is similar to that made for deceit during wartime. Because ordinary channels of correction have broken down and law and morality cannot be successfully used, then "more primitive" principles must be brought into play—justifying such action with the rationale that "all is fair in love and war."

Although such arguments are sometimes to the point, Bok says, they are likely to be only rationalizations. Obscuring reasoning, they invite bias, exaggerate the crisis at hand and the motives of the opponents, and fail to consider the adequacy of other investigative methods. The idea that anyone serious about investigative reporting must use disguise and deceit is, for Bok, one of the most serious ethical concerns in journalism. Even if a group of journalists concludes that no alternative means are available for investigating a certain problem, they must, according to Bok, "still weigh the moral arguments for and against deceptive infiltration or other surreptitious methods."

Sissela Bok calls for thoughtfulness, seriousness, a sense of justice and fairness, and a deep sense of journalistic honesty and personal integrity. She finds it encouraging that the press stands for openness in public discourse. But she warns that until journalists firmly support openness in their own practices, their image will be flawed and their credibility lessened. Journalists should welcome criticism and close observation of their work; their own secrecy, investigative techniques, and selective disclosure should never be excluded from scrutiny. Bok concludes her insightful and wise words for the journalist with this observation: "Because the task of reporting the news is both an indispensable public resource and big business, and because of the great power now wielded by the media, a commitment to openness and to accountability is more necessary than ever."

[31]

A FEW MORE BRIEF LEGACIES

Perhaps on these closing pages a few more intellectual leaders should be mentioned. So let us briefly add to the legacy of wisdom, starting back several centuries before the Christian era, with the legacy of Buddha.

GAUTAMA THE BUDDHA

Among the early figures that influenced society was Gautama the Buddha (c. 563–483 B.C.). The Buddhist journalist would be one who had no desire to compete, to change things, to love materialism, to strive, or to conform to the world. An attempt to promote "progress" or to "leave the world a better place"—pragmatic concepts that seem to permeate modern journalism—would be meaningless to the follower of Gautama the Buddha.

Buddhist journalists would have a serene detachment from the world, would participate in daily life without being drawn into it. Whether they could be journalists with such an attitude is doubtful. For the follower of Buddha—a person of gentleness, serenity, and peace—the only thing worth seeking is the bliss of Nirvana.

Whereas most foundational mentors for the journalist stress self-enhancement and self-knowledge, Buddha urged extinction of the self. And like most gurus of India, he placed great significance on meditation, emptying oneself of all thoughts and distractions. He taught that neither the pleasures of the world nor ascetic mortification of the flesh is the correct way to live. His teaching was mainly confined to what he called the Noble Eightfold Path, which can be capsulized as: right views, right aspiration, right speech, right conduct, right means of livelihood, right endeavor, right mindfulness, and right concentration. Buddhists are enjoined to be truthful, refrain from strong drink, and not harm any creature. They are also taught to follow the four modes of inner conduct: loving-kindness, compassion, sympathetic joy, and equanimity. Buddha also taught gentleness, non-violence, compassion, and respect for all life.

Even metaphysical speculation, in Buddhist teaching, is to be avoided; such thinking is harmful because it leads to quarrels and controversies, from which a person must be freed. Such philosophical questioning as advocated by Socrates does nothing for the Buddhist; it actually impedes one's progress along the road to Nirvana. In this belief in the non-necessity of rational intellectualizing, Buddhism is similar to Christianity. Even though the Western journalist may not feel comfortable with the extinction of the self concept in Buddhism, he or she can surely find beneficial the inner peace, gentleness, respect for life, and tolerance that Gautama the Buddha taught.

FYODOR DOSTOEVSKY

Moving a long way toward the present and into the Western World, one finds Fyodor Dostoevsky (1821–1881) preoccupied with the implications of freedom in all his works. In this area, he has much to say to the modern journalist. Especially in his novella *Notes from the Underground* and the "Grand Inquisitor" section of *The Brothers Karama-*

zov, he deals with freedom and its consequences. In both, Dostoevsky tries to solve the problem of the truly free individual who must live in harmony with the social order. He is trying to understand free will in relation to ethical choices; this, in a nutshell, is the prime quandary of the modern journalist.

Although Dostoevsky has been called the precursor to existentialism, his Underground Man evidences clearly the pitfalls of unexamined existentialism. He defiantly rejects all appeals to rational self-interest, which he sees as a travesty of human dignity. The Underground Man is offended at a conception of man as a rational, therefore predictable, person, left with no freedom and no will of his own. Against such a society in which action is so rationally conducted that all adventure is lost, the Underground Man rebels. He is a kind of anti-hero whose chaotic existence points up the need for a positive ethical ideal. The modern journalist needs to consider carefully such a need.

The Underground Man, forsaking the laws of society, is certainly a person enjoying maximum freedom. This story says that such freedom imposes a tremendous responsibility on the person making such a choice. Journalists who live by their own creeds are no less responsible for their actions than those who conform to rules handed to them as guides to social responsibility. In fact, as with the Underground Man, such freely choosing journalists are even more responsible because they have personally formed their own creeds. Perhaps the lesson for the journalist is that he or she must create an ethical framework in which free will can operate without psychological damage to the self or social damage to others.

In the Grand Inquisitor section of *The Brothers Karamazov,* his final novel written in 1880, Dostoevsky is probably at his best in grappling with the problem of freedom. The Grand Inquisitor is a warning against social conformity, which is seen to be just as terrible as unprincipled freedom. During the Spanish Inquisition, Dostoevsky has Christ visit Seville as the fiery Inquisition rages. He is put in jail by the Inquisitor who proceeds to explain to him that people do not want to be free, that freedom is nothing but a burden to them. What humanity wants is a guided society of order and stability. This position is the opposite of that of Christ and to some degree the Underground Man, who asserts that what people want is free choice regardless of where such choice may lead and what it may cost.

Just whom Dostoevsky was siding with (the Inquisitor or Christ?) has long been a matter of speculation, but because he was a Christian we may infer that it was Christ. As for the modern journalist looking at the story, he or she can either accept the Inquisitor's position—that society (and journalism) needs authority and that freedom is extravagant and disruptive—or take Christ's position—that humanity should be free, even though such a state may be traumatic and dangerous.

LOUIS D. BRANDEIS

One of America's foremost jurists, Louis D. Brandeis (1856–1941), was a thinker who is often overlooked or placed somewhere in the shadow of his better-known colleague, Oliver Wendell Holmes. Brandeis has much to say to the journalist about courage, truth, and honesty and is considered the father of the concept of privacy (first discussed by him and Samuel Warren in a *Harvard Law Review* article in December 1890). This privacy concept established the framework for a person's right to be left alone, a complex legal (and moral) idea. Brandeis would always wrestle with the fine balance between a person's privacy and the press's right to publish, a problem journalists still face every day.

Brandeis' Supreme Court tenure (1916–39) was a mixture of social reform, defense of Jeffersonian principles of free speech, and promotion of many of his own causes. Whereas Holmes—

his friend, court colleague, and former teacher at Harvard—is usually portrayed as the philosopher, Brandeis is thought of as the pragmatist. This is rather strange because Brandeis' opinions usually constituted a far deeper exploration of fact, social substance, and ramifications. Brandeis believed in absolute truth; Holmes did not, being a utilitarian as exemplified by his idea of the "marketplace of ideas." Holmes had no practical understanding as to good and bad laws, except as he compared them to "what the crowd wants." Brandeis knew, or thought he knew, what good and bad laws (and ideas) were.

Brandeis generally agreed with Holmes' "clear and present danger test" (restricting press freedom during wartime and crisis) but was always cautious about its application during peacetime when an "intolerant majority" might well call "disloyal" any opinion with which it disagreed. But as much as Brandeis loved the concepts of free speech and free press, he was always plagued by the paradox of such freedom interfering with the individual's freedom. Privacy for the person vis-à-vis government was much clearer to him than was privacy in the press context.

Although press freedom was important to Brandeis, his greatest contribution to legal theory is undoubtedly the idea that people had a right to be left alone by government. He called this the most comprehensive of rights and "the one most valued by civilized men." In his *Olmstead v. U.S.* opinion (1928), writing about the right to privacy, he said, "To protect that right, every unjustifiable intrusion upon the privacy of the individual, whatever the means employed, must be deemed a violation of the Fourth Amendment." This is blunt language. But it was typical of the courageous and absolutist mind of one of America's greatest Supreme Court justices.

H. L. MENCKEN

Shifting now from the legal world to the media world, we come to a titan among the versatile journalists of America. Any journalist who is not thin-skinned and who welcomes some sharp-edged criticism will find H. L. Mencken (1880–1956) and his pull-no-punches brand of journalism interesting, and maybe even helpful. During Mencken's half century as an editor, reporter, columnist, and editorial writer, mainly for the Baltimore *Sun* little escaped his keen observation and scathing criticism.

He was the author of six important books of criticism and language *(A Book of Prefaces* and *The American Language* being the best representatives) and was at work on two memoirs at the time of his death: *Thirty-Five Years of Newspaper Work, 1906–41* and *My Life as Author and Editor,* both of which appeared in the mid-1990s. From 1924 to 1933 Mencken edited *The American Mercury,* arguably the most important magazine published in America at the time. And with George Jean Nathan he co-edited *The Smart Set;* it was in this capacity that he met and influenced many literary figures, among them Theodore Dreiser, Willa Cather, Sinclair Lewis, F. Scott Fitzgerald, Eugene O'Neill, Lewis Mumford, Maxwell Anderson, Ben Hecht, and Dorothy Parker.

It was while Mencken was on the staff of the Baltimore *Sun* papers that he wrote his most scathing comments about journalism and journalists. The book of his edited essays that best presents his barbed critique is *A Gang of Pecksniffs,* edited by Theo Lippman Jr. Although he was a curmudgeon, he had a great sense of humor and seldom showed malice. He simply avoided people he disliked. His writing philosophy was: "Stir up the animals." And such a philosophy produced volumes of venomous work. He had little use for the so-called balanced, fair editorial and felt that people wanted to read outrageous and colorful criticism. This he consistently provided.

According to Mencken the average American newspaper was ignorant, unfair, hypocritical, perfidious, lewd, and dishonest. And journalists were mainly inept, relying on formula writing and shying away from courageous and honest reporting. Journalism schools also came in for his biting comments: "Probably half of them, indeed, are simply refuges for students too stupid to tackle the other professions."

Journalists have little freedom, said Mencken. They are merely hirelings and must answer to those above them; they sell their services to editors, publishers, and business managers—not to the public. And what further reduces their autonomy is their tendency to swallow propaganda from the wire services and government without searching for the real story. But Mencken had one basic journalistic belief that most modern journalists would agree with: Journalists should fight for the limitation of government powers and for the greatest possible press freedom.

Mencken was a solid writer, keen observer, and versatile and courageous critic. The modern journalist might well imitate his love of learning and communication skills.

DAVID RIESMAN

Now we turn to an American writer with a more oblique style than Mencken's and one who exemplifies the sociological connections with journalism: David Riesman (1909–). He published, with Nathan Glazer and Reuel Denney, *The Lonely Crowd: A Study of the Changing American Character,* perhaps the first scholarly book to examine closely America's growing conformity, consumerism, and complacency. In it, Riesman argued that the mass media were strongly accelerating a decline in both individualism and community. Such critiques are common today, but at mid-century little attention was being paid to a nexus of society and the mass media.

Riesman was trained at Harvard as a biochemist and lawyer; he was not formally educated as a sociologist. He worked for a decade as a trial lawyer, law professor, and deputy assistant district attorney before he got a teaching appointment in 1946 in the social sciences at the University of Chicago. He taught there until 1958 when he left to teach at Harvard, from which he retired in 1980.

In *The Lonely Crowd,* Riesman argues that societies develop in three ways: (1) tradition-directed, (2) inner-directed, and (3) other-directed. Although he was dealing with societies and their development and characteristics, his typology has sometimes been related to individuals, and that could mean journalists. In the media there are the traditionalists, who need to obey and follow rules and respect the way things have been done in the past. And there are the self-directed journalists, who, with an existential orientation, try to increase personal autonomy in their work. Finally, there are those journalists who succumb to the pressures and wishes of other people, such as colleagues in the media or other potent opinion-making constituencies. These would be the journalists, who in Riesman's scheme, would be part of the "lonely crowd."

Riesman's ideas can also be considered in the context of societies. For example, in other-directed societies the mass media would try to please their audiences, give the people what they want, and have their agenda set primarily by actual or potential audience members. Or they could, in authoritarian societies, mainly attempt to please the ruler or dominant party. Here the journalistic agenda would not deal with moral issues or personal growth but rather with the expectations and dictates of popular culture.

The modern journalist can learn much from Riesman, not only from his societal typologies but also from his discussion of the tendencies toward conformity in modern cultures. As people seek to become more like each other, he says, they lose their individual autonomy and social freedom. Riesman believes that most people, the other-directed ones, depend too heavily on social direction; they need to divorce themselves from the agenda of others, opt out of the lonely crowd, and reassert their individualism and self-enhancement. This may well be a good tip for today's "corporate" journalists, who are, in a very real sense, alienated in the midst of machinelike journalism.

MARTIN BUBER

One of the modern world's most prominent Jewish thinkers, one that put interpersonal communication on the throne of importance, was Martin Buber (1878–1965). Like Socrates, Buber would admonish us to know ourselves but would mean that we must form what he called an I–Thou relationship with another in order to do this.

When the journalist, for example, talks about responsibility, he or she has to be thinking of a relationship with others. The journalist cannot be responsible alone or in non-personal situations. Responsibility must have a personal object; ultimately it must be considered in the context of consequences to others. Buber's best-known work, *I and Thou* (1923), deals with this concept. Later books, such as *Between Man and Man* (translated into English in 1965), also deal with this theme.

In the journalistic context, a responsible journalism demands both a subject and an object—an I and a Thou. There must be the actor (journalist) and a person or people acted upon (audience). Of course, in journalism it is difficult and often impossible to develop this I–Thou relationship because of the general anonymity of the communicants. Buber would probably say that it is not likely that such social intercourse can occur in the journalistic context. So, in a real sense, in mass communication the real essence of communication cannot come about; only a very superficial or peripheral communication can result.

Buber is in favor of a "free market" of discourse, a diversity of perspectives. Certainly journalism can help provide this. People, however, should present their positions and ideas in an empathic and considerate way; no shouting at one another, name-calling, or simply talking to one's self. Editorial writers and columnists, especially, should take note. Here was Buber, an existentialist, who was not satisfied to live within himself; he saw the need for social interaction, for establishing bridges between and among people. However, Buber is quick to point out the danger to a person in a collectivistic undertaking. He didn't use the word, but perhaps he would prefer the term communitarian to collectivistic. In a *community* one relates more to others; in a *collective* one becomes anonymous and selfless. And no existentialist would want to opt for anonymity and selflessness.

Martin Buber, educated at universities in Vienna, Berlin, Leipzig, and Zurich, was at one time editor of Vienna's *Die Welt,* a Zionist journal. From 1916 until 1924 he edited *Der Jude,* a leading voice of German-speaking Jews. During the Nazi rise to power he taught at the University of Frankfurt, leaving in 1938 for Jerusalem where, until his death, he was a philosophy professor at Hebrew University. His is a journalistic legacy of true communication.

I. F. STONE

Standing alongside H. L. Mencken as one of America's leading examples of skeptical, searching, insightful, and independent journalism was I. F. Stone (1907–1989). In fact, he may well be the country's *most* independent, and certainly one of the most "radical" (as he called himself), reporters. His newsletter, *I. F. Stone's Weekly,* was a prime example of political reporting and media criticism. And it exemplified just how much effect one dedicated person, using only a small non-establishment publication, can have on social thinking.

Stone was born Isidor "Izzy" Feinstein in New Jersey and, growing up in the town of Haddonfield, early immersed himself in poetry, politics, and philosophy. A lover of ancient Greek thought, Stone developed an ethical philosophy that mixed the concepts of Plato and Aristotle with that of Immanuel Kant, whose categorical imperative always impressed him. Throughout his life he had a reverence for the power of words and the importance of accepting responsibility for actions and a sense of duty to principle—all of which he felt should direct the work of the journalist.

Stone was especially hard on any limitation on the independence of a reporter. Integrity in reporting was for him extremely important, and this could not occur when a reporter was directed and controlled by others. Historical context was, for Stone, the essence of a good news report, and he always stressed the importance of careful research and documentation. He placed the responsibility for avoiding ethical compromises on the press itself, although he recognized the temptation and pressures faced by journalists in covering government.

He bemoaned the fact that the press was largely motivated by profit rather than principle and was especially critical of the danger that advertising poses to journalistic autonomy. But he was equally determined to stay independent of readers, believing that a journalist can be enslaved by the expectations of the audience. The real test of journalistic courage and leadership, he believed, is whether a journalist is willing to support causes unpopular with the readers. Although Stone was a life-long socialist and a leader in left-wing politics, he would, from time to time, antagonize his liberal readers with certain of his perspectives. One of his best writings dealing with the subject of freedom of expression was his book *The Trial of Socrates,* in which he bemoaned the Athenian democracy that put the great philosopher to death.

Certainly a controversial figure, with many critics as well as admirers, I. F. Stone helps provide modern journalism with a legacy of personal involvement, radical activism, a firm belief in deontological ethics, a love of freedom, and a willingness to take chances and accept personal responsibility.

ALBERT CAMUS

This proclivity for freedom and personal responsibility was exemplified in Europe by Albert Camus (1913–1960), a thinker who well combined the intellectual interests of the philosopher with the practical inclinations of the journalist. This French (born and raised in Algeria) novelist, essayist, and journalist exemplifies the extreme love of freedom and personal development common to the existential tradition to which he belonged. In 1938 he was working as a journalist for several newspapers in Algeria and France, and during the German occupation of France during World War II, he was active in the French underground press.

Camus, although he didn't call himself one, was a freewheeling existentialist, evidencing in his articles vigor yet restraint, anguish yet hope, historical perspective yet future orientation, individualism yet social awareness. He had a deep respect for facts, coupled with thoughtful subjectivity. He was part mystical artist and part public-conscious social scientist. During the bleak days of World War II, his Parisian newspaper *Combat* was a source of information and encouragement for the anti-Nazi resistance. Later, after the war, Camus continued in journalism by writing for the serious Paris weekly *L'Express,* and at the time of his death in an automobile accident, he was writing for many French newspapers.

What are the main traits of a good journalist? Camus' answer went something like this: a deep concern and respect for self and others, and for the truth; and a desire for social progress and personal involvement, coupled with a sense of responsibility, personal commitment, and a deep love of freedom. Camus valued the rebel, but he realized that rebellion, like freedom, implies danger and often isolation. And maturity demands realism and moderation, qualities Camus believed are the prime requirements for good journalism.

As was true of Nietzsche, Camus would say yea, not only to life, but to freedom and responsibility. Freedom would come first, perhaps, but he firmly believed that the journalist should be willing to accept personal responsibility for every action—a basic existentialist tenet also promulgated by Jean-Paul Sartre, Simone de Beauvoir, and other existentialist writers. Unlike his fellow existentialist Sartre, however, Camus would seek to change society indirectly through the individual journalist's efforts to change himself or herself. Sartre, more overtly community-minded, would directly change the conditions of people's lives in order to change them individually. Camus was more inner-directed, Sartre more other-directed.

Camus would say the journalist should mainly be concerned with the present, with the practical needs of the moment, because the journalist pays attention mainly to the self; although struggle against others may be necessary, emphasis should be on self-development and the persuasion of others. Sartre, on the other hand, believed in a more forceful role—to assist directly in bringing about needed changes through strong government action, if necessary.

Camus deeply valued the traits of authenticity, self-development, honesty, openness, the freedom to choose, and the creation of an aesthetic order. Believing in change, as did Sartre, Camus would see it as more evolutionary than revolutionary. One important trait of the existentialist in journalism is self-respect. And this is related to ethically oriented freedom that should result in providing a wide range of information and pluralism of viewpoints that have a positive social effect. The freedom-loving individualist in the journalist will find a kindred spirit in Albert Camus.

HANNAH ARENDT

The eminent philosopher Hannah Arendt (1906–1975) was a native of Hannover, Germany, and the only child of German-Jewish parents. She studied philosophy under the great Karl Jaspers at Heidelberg and received her doctorate in 1928. As the Nazis came to power in 1933, Arendt fled to France and soon emigrated to the United States, where she was an innovative political theorist and teacher at several American universities until her retirement.

Her best-known work is *The Origins of Totalitarianism* (1951), in which she deals with the rise of repressive movements in Russia and Germany. She speaks of "organized loneliness" as contributing to such totalitarianism; this, as she saw it, was not solitude, but a situation in which individuals lose contact with the world and one another. There is no shared worldview among people, and without such a view, people lack a "common sense" and an ability to know the difference between fiction and reality. They therefore become easily manipulated by a totalitarian ideology. She wrote many books, including *The Human Condition* (1958), *Eichmann in Jerusalem* (1963), *Men in Dark Times* (1968), and *The Life of the Mind* (1978, two volumes, published posthumously).

Arendt would tell the journalist that evil lurks at every turn. For her this is a kind of thoughtlessness, a shallowness or the inability to realize what one is doing. In the hustle of daily journalism, such a thoughtlessness or shallowness is omnipresent, constantly impinging on the ethical decisions that must be made in quick succession. What happens to the journalist is what easily occurs in an authoritarian society: A person becomes remote from reality and denies a connectedness to others. Such radical wickedness, according to Arendt, is a kind of defect, or perhaps a disease, of imagination.

The ethical journalist would be, in Arendt's view, a person who recognizes the force of evil ("the shame of being human . . . the inescapable guilt of the human race") and can really fight against it. It is that fight, she said, injecting an existentialist tone, that gives meaning to a person's life. Arendt, like many of the other great thinkers discussed in this book, was a firm believer in freedom. Especially dear to her was freedom of expression. Acting out of this freedom, she would tell the journalist, is essential for a meaningful journalism. Like the historian Barbara Tuchman, Arendt would have the journalist be a creative artist, bringing adventure and meaning to a piece of writing. And like Martin Buber, she would have this artist connect with others to create a moral community.

Arendt's advice to journalists: connect with others, constantly fight the evil that surrounds you, think and write like an artist, prize freedom and work to extend its boundaries, and take action in the name of freedom and justice. In other words, Arendt would tell the journalist to maximize his or her human potency by thinking well, writing well, and expanding the civility and well-being of the social group.

EPILOGUE

We have now presented the legacy of wisdom passed down to today's journalists. It is incomplete, of course, and there are many great thinkers who are missing from these pages. But those who are here form an impressive group of men and women who have much to contribute to the journalist and student.

There are many thinkers who are not included in these pages but who have influenced my thinking and surely have much to say about today's journalism. The interested reader might consider exploring the work of some of the following: Thomas Jefferson, Benjamin Franklin, James Madison, Ibn Khaldun, G.W.F. Hegel, Friedrich Nietzsche, Jean-Paul Sartre, Arnold Toynbee, Reinhold Niebuhr, Carl Jung, Oliver Wendell Holmes, Walter Lippmann, John Dewey, Sigmund Freud, Henry David Thoreau, Jean-Jacques Rousseau, Mahatma Gandhi, Neil Postman, José Ortega y Gasset, George Santayana, Rabindranath Tagore, Bertrand Russell, Karl Jaspers, Erich Fromm, Karl Popper, Leo Strauss, and Robert Nozick.

Getting acquainted with such intellectual giants of past and present is a great adventure, one that is particularly rich and meaningful for people who are in or plan to enter the important field of journalism. The concourse of ideas offered as a legacy stretches in all directions and is accessible to the curious student and thoughtful journalist. This great body of wisdom, only hinted at in this slim volume, stands quietly waiting to be let in. I hope you will open the door.

GLOSSARY

ALTRUISM. In ethics usually seen in opposition to egoism; altruists claim that morality cannot be reduced to self-interest, that it must take the interest of other people into consideration; emphasis is on others, not on one's self.

AUTHENTIC. In the existential sense, being one's true self; living up to one's potential; lack of hypocrisy; shunning false appearances.

AUTHORITARIANISM. In journalism, a press system controlled by the government, or journalists deprived of freedom or autonomy.

AXIOLOGY. The philosophical study of values; includes aesthetics and ethics.

CAPITALISTIC PRESS. Private ownership of media; implies media competition and press pluralism; profit motive is important.

CATEGORICAL IMPERATIVE. Kant's test for ethical maxims: Do only those things you would will to see universalized.

COLLECTIVISTIC PRESS. Socialistic media; owned and directed by party-government apparatus; no privately owned media; a form of authoritanism in journalism.

COMMUNITARIANISM. In ethics, emphasizing the community and common interest; opposed to individualism and classical liberalism; journalism should solidify the community, not fractionalize it; absolutist ethics needed for social harmony and cohesion; reluctance to publish stories that might fractionalize society; desire to bring social harmony through "positive" journalism; de-emphasizing older Enlightenment liberalism of journalistic autonomy.

CONSCIENCE. Convictions or values held by a person, used for moral guidance; when moral beliefs provide strong motivation for acting in a certain way, this set of beliefs is often called "conscience." Considered "voice of God" by some.

CONSEQUENTIALISM. Umbrella term for ethical theories stating that rightness or wrongness of an action is dependent on the results the action produces; a variation on this would be the anticipated or intended results; also called teleological ethics; most popular version—utilitarian ethics.

CORRESPONDENCE THEORY OF TRUTH. Truth is agreement with reality; the correspondence between a statement and the way things actually are. Truth, as in a news story, is relational; the statements correspond to reality, to a fact; the usual test for truth or accuracy in journalism.

DEONTOLOGY. In ethics, law or maxim-oriented; duty-ethics; follow a priori ethical principles and not be concerned with consequences; best example of a deontologist—Immanuel Kant. Contrasted to teleological (consquentialist) ethics.

DIALECTIC. A clash of ideas or extremes (thesis and antithesis) merging (into a synthesis), forming a more moderate or more advanced (in Hegelian sense) position.

EGALITARIANISM. In ethics, a desire to achieve equality among people, at least equality of opportunity; in journalism, treating all people similarly.

EGOISTIC ETHICS. Using self as the moral reference point; determining ethical norms and actions without reference to outside considerations; concern with self-development and self-determination; in ethical sense, using reason for personal growth and development of character; rests on the hypothesis that morality can be ultimately explained in terms of self-interest, albeit so-called (e.g., Ayn Rand) "enlightened self-interest"; what is in a person's own self-interest ultimately determines what is in the interest of society.

EMOTIVE THEORY OF ETHICS. View that ethical terms do not describe anything, but are only expressions of the feelings of the person using them; for example, the utterance of "X is good" is no more than saying "I like X." An ethical statement, then, is no more than a report of a person's emotional state, or attitude.

ENLIGHTENMENT. 18th century European liberal emphasis on reason, individualism, and freedom; also known as the Age of Reason.

EPISTEMOLOGY. Study of knowledge; in journalism, a concern with getting at the truth; nature of objectivity; the nature and derivation of knowledge; getting and verification of information.

ETHICS. Generally suggests a set of standards by which a person or group decides to regulate its behavior; hence we refer to journalism ethics.

EXISTENTIALISM. A philosophical trend or attitude as distinct from a dogma or system; origin attributed to Kierkegaard. Became influential in continental Europe in second quarter of 20th century with writings of Jaspers, Heiddeger, Marcel, Sartre and Camus. Stresses "authentic" living—preservation of a person's individual identity under social demands; emphasis also on individual freedom, action, and acceptance of personal responsibility. A person "makes" the self (really exists) through action and self-awareness; existential stance of freedom and acton based on self-direction and responsibility.

FREEDOM. Positive and negative: terms introduced by Isaiah Berlin to make a distinction between the sort of freedom ("negative freedom") that one has when not prevented from doing what one wants to do, and that sort of freedom ("positive freedom") that lies in actually doing something with one's freedom.

GOLDEN MEAN. A philosophy of moderation in a person's life, as discussed by Aristotle who saw it as the rational and virtuous course between extremes of excess; also strongly advocated by Confucius.

HEDONISM. Belief that happiness—pleasure—is the highest good.

HUMANISM. A term with a wide variety of rather vague meanings; two most important conceptions: (1) intellectual movement of Renaissance in Europe that stressed cultures of classical Greece and Rome; spirit of optimism about human possibilities, enthusiastic about human achievements; consistent with a belief in God, and (2) in 20th century another meaning developed by those who reject all religious beliefs, insisting on concern only for human welfare in this, allegedly, the only world; often called "secular humanism."

IDEALISM. A philosophical view (e.g., Plato's) that an "ideal" (perfect idea) exists somewhere for every concrete entity; these things we see are only imperfect representations or manifestations of the perfect or ideal thing; a philosophy of hope, of human striving toward perfection; a belief in personal and social progress toward the perfect or ideal; often contrasted with realism—a more mundane and materialistic perspective.

IDEOLOGY. Generally used for any system of ideas and norms directing political and social action; e.g., "Marxist ideology" or "libertarian ideology."

INTUITIONISM. In ethics, the view that (at least some) moral judgments are known to be true by intuition; that a kind of mystical, non-rational sense or feeling informs our moral decisions.

JUSTICE. A basic concept in ethics having to do with providing the proper results to people; being fair; often considered as providing equality of judgment or even the equality of outcome; deservedness.

LIBERTARIANISM. A view opposed to determinism that human actions are not—or not entirely—governed by causal laws. In journalism, the emphasis on editorial autonomy of the press or the journalist; no prior censorship; wholehearted liberalism, opposed to authoritarian restraints on individual freedom; not always synonymous with liberalism today.

NIHILISM. Nothingness; main values, belief in nothing other than materialism, science, revolution; usually associated with destructiveness and radicalism.

NORMATIVE ETHICS. Also called prescriptive ethics; unlike meta-ethics which is restricted to analysis of moral terms (like "right" and "good"), normative ethics tries to give a rational basis for judgments about what is right or good; any system dictating morally correct conduct.

OBJECTIVISM. The idea that meaningful and reasonably accurate statements can be made about reality; opposite of subjectivism or idealism; reality is sufficiently describable and justifiable to rational people; in journalism (objectivity), the concept of neutrality where the journalist tries to be dispassionate, precise, thorough, and factually oriented, omitting personal opinions, judgments and biases. In ethics, the belief that there are certain moral truths that would remain true whatever anyone thought about them.

RATIONALISM. In a narrow sense, the doctrines of a group of philosophers of the 17th and 18th centuries, e.g., Descartes, Spinoza, and Liebnitz; in a wider sense, using reason alone to learn about existence, that everything is explainable; a belief only in what has a rational foundation—can be held up to the careful scrutiny of reason.

RELATIVISM. In ethics (e.g., Aristotle) the idea that right and wrong vary from place to place; relativist recognizes the importance of social context in determining what ought to be the case; also the circumstances or specific situation; to be an ethical relativist is to maintain that there are no universal standards of good and bad, right or wrong. For example, Joseph Fletcher's "situation ethics" is relativistic in that what is ethical is relative to Christian love (*agape*).

SEMANTICS. The study of meaning; general semantics—the study of how symbols (words, language) affect thought and action.

SEMIOTICS. Theory of signs; semiology; includes semantics, syntactics (study of grammar) and pragmatics (study of the actual purposes and effects of meaning of utterances).

SITUATIONALISM. In ethics, taking the specific situation into consideration in making moral decisions; a relativistic stance contrasted to absolute or universal ethics.

SKEPTICISM. Doubting; contrasted with "dogmatic"; uncertainty, suspicious.

STOICISM. In ethics, morality that is rigorously naturalistic—the best way to live is to live consistently and harmoniously with nature; reason is important to show what our nature is so we can do the appropriate things; commonly used as a term indicating a personal inclination to persist in trouble calmly; imperturbability, with passive dignity, a kind of inner freedom to be attained through submission to providence and a detachment from everything not in our power (example: the teaching of Epictetus (c. 60–130 A.D.).

SUBJECTIVISM. In ethics, the belief that all moral attitudes are merely a matter of personal opinion or taste; in journalism generally, the injection of personal opinion or bias into a story; straying away from hard facts and neutral depiction of reality.

TELEOLOGY. In ethics, consequentialist; ethical action to be determined by the actual consequences or the prediction of consequences; contrasted to deontology (the following of a priori rules or maxims).

TRANSCENDENTALISM. A mode of thought emphasizing the intuitive and supersensuous; a religious sensibility; a reaction against dogmatic rationalism.

UTILITARIANISM. In ethics, associated with Jeremy Bentham, J. S. Mill, and Henry Sidgwick; basically a form of teleological (consequentialism) ethics, specifically accepting as the foundation of ethics Utility or the Greatest Happiness principle; actions are right or wrong as they tend to promote happiness (pleasure) or pain (or the privation of pleasure).

ABOUT THE AUTHOR

John C. Merrill is professor emeritus of journalism at the University of Missouri–Columbia. He taught at Missouri from 1964 to 1979, leaving for 11 years to teach at the University of Maryland and Louisiana State University. He returned to Columbia in 1992 and teaches graduate seminars there. He has taught journalism, English, and philosophy, reflecting his own education: a bachelor's degree in English and history, two master's degrees (in journalism and in philosophy), and a doctorate in mass communications from the University of Iowa.

He has also been a newspaper reporter, feature writer, wire editor, and columnist and has lectured, conducted workshops, and led conferences around the world.

Merrill is the author of some 20 books, most of them in the areas of journalism, philosophy, mass communication and society, and international communication. They include *The Foreign Press, The Elite Press, International Communication, The Imperative of Freedom, Existential Journalism, The Dialectic in Journalism, Macromedia* (with Ralph Lowenstein), and *Media Debates* (with Everette Dennis).

Merrill has been a senior fellow at the Freedom Forum Media Studies Center at Columbia University, has received the Distinguished Service Award in International Communication from the Association of Education in Journalism and Mass Communication (AEJMC), the Trayes Outstanding Faculty Award (given annually by AEJMC), the Lifetime Service Award (given by the University of Missouri School of Journalism), and the Distinguished Research Master award (given each year to one person campuswide by Louisiana State University) and is a member of the Journalism Hall of Fame at Louisiana State University.